CHARACTER DANCE

CHARACTER DANCE

Jurgen Pagels

INDIANA UNIVERSITY PRESS • BLOOMINGTON

Manufactured in the United States of America

Library of Congress Cataloging in Publication Data

Pagels, Jurgen, 1925–
Character dance.

Translated from the German.
Bibliography: p.
1. Ballet dancing.   2. Folk dancing.   I. Title.
GV1788.P33   1984   792.8'2   82–49013
ISBN 0–253–31337–6
1 2 3 4 5 88 87 86 85 84

Contents

ILLUSTRATIONS

PREFACE

During the years I have lived in the United States, my teaching and performing experiences in the ballet world and in theatre generally have brought me to the realization that a comprehensive guideline for class instruction of character and national dance is urgently needed. This volume is intended as a reference source for teachers and students of all types of dance, whether on a professional performance level or on an amateur recreational level. A knowledge of character dance is a valuable addition to all other acquired styles and disciplines of dance. I stress that the following material is to be used as a reference. A complete analysis of the often difficult technical requirements and an in-depth description of the historical background of each dance would be painstakingly lengthy. I therefore have limited myself to a technique for daily instruction in the classroom or on the stage, for observation or participation.

The reader does not need previous experience with systems of dance notation (Benesch or Laban, e.g.), and it is difficult to translate dance steps into words. Therefore, where possible, I have adhered to the classical ballet positioning of the legs and arms, but these positions should be interpreted loosely. Note that some steps are notated by their native or common name, while others are given in a translation from the original language. Classical ballet terms are explained in more detail in the Glossary. For further reference see Gail Grant, *Technical Manual and Dictionary of Classical Ballet*, available from Dover Publishers, Inc., 180 Varick Street, New York, NY 10014.

Records for the barre exercises can be purchased from Taffy's, 701 Beta Drive, Cleveland, OH 44143 and other dance outfitters. The Mazurka, Csárdás, and Betrothal Dance are from the ballet *Coppélia* by Leo Delibes. Use the complete recording conducted by Ansermet (on the London label). Music for the Tarantella is from the ballet *La Boutique Fantasque* by Rossini/Respighi. The Trepak is from the ballet *The Nutcracker* by Tchaikovsky. Many recordings present the ballet as a suite and include the Trepak. The Polka is from the opera *The Bartered Bride* by Smetana. All these records are available in most record stores.

ACKNOWLEDGMENTS

My special thanks go to my former teachers and friends in this particular form of dance, without whose knowledge and instruction it would not have been possible to write this treatise or to pass on to others the dance traditions of many hundreds of years: To Jo Mensebach, formerly of the Luebeck Opera House, Germany; to Valentine Prorvitch, formerly of the Bolshoi Theater, Moscow; to Oscar Harmoš, former chief choreographer of the Yugoslav National Ballet; and to the late Eizens Lesčevskis, balletmaster of the Riga National Ballet Company. I am also grateful to Indiana University and to its School of Music for support in this undertaking; to Sandra Kowadla for the drawings; to Laurel Lampton for posing for the photos; to Deborah Martin, pianist; and to Colin Russell for general assistance.

Introduction

What Is Character Dance?

Originally based on folklore, but refined and adapted for stage usage, character dance has played a major role in the production of many traditional classical ballets. These include *Swan Lake*, with Neapolitan, Spanish, Polish, and Hungarian dances; *Sleeping Beauty*, with a Polonaise; and *Coppélia*, with a Mazurka and a Csárdás. As the word *character* implies, this type of dance is a portrayal of certain individual characteristics—the way the body is held, the arm movements, and the head carriage. Often the body displays a highly individual personification: an old, funny, miserly, or eccentric man; or perhaps a robust, seductive, but good-humored woman. The characterization is used in a broad sense to cover not the individual but an entire range of national attributes. For the sake of authenticity one must analyze, study, and fully comprehend the various characteristics of each step and of each nationality. Too often a mixture of various steps and styles from different nations are put together in a potpourri of movement and labeled "Russian." The choreographer must keep the authenticity of a dance in mind, so as not to lose the true spirit of the national dance required.

There is no doubt that folklore and sophisticated ballroom techniques have had a great influence on today's stage dance. Certain forms, formations, and steps have prevailed—such as skips, hops, and galops; the two-step; the Polkas, Waltzes, and Mazurkas—that provide a definite link between folk, national, and character dance. Consider the *pas de basque*. The name reveals that it is a step of the Basques, from the region of the western Pyrenees on the Franco-Spanish border; yet many other countries perform the same step in their dances and call it by another name. There is a certain initial similarity in execution but a difference in character, be it the way the legs move sideways or up and down, the way the arms are held and move, or the way the head tilts. The same can be said of many other steps, from the ordinary skip, the *ballonnés* and *ballottés* of the Italian Tarantella, to the *chassé* of the classical technique. The harmonica-like movement of the Russian Gormoshka appeared in the Big Apple of the 1920s. The heel clicking Bokazo reappeared in the Charleston and in jazz ballet.

Looking back into dance history, we find many examples of character dance used on its

1

own account or translated into classical technique. Bournonville used the Neapolitan dance in his choreography. Fanny Elssler was renowned for her Spanish Cacchucha and Polish Krakowiak. The Russian dancer Bekeffi was credited with an apparently successful introduction of national dances on the Russian ballet stage in 1880. Many great classical ballets of that period and of later years have made use of character dances.

The 1920s in Russia found pupils in daily character dance classes, based on a syllabus worked out by Alexander Shiryaev. The larger and more reputable dance academies in Europe have since followed suit and have national and character dance in their weekly schedules. Instrumental in spreading the gospel was Serge Diaghilev's Ballet Russe, which dominated the Western world from 1909 to the company's demise in 1929. Originally, Diaghilev's presentation was confined to Russian painting and opera. But the Parisians were so impressed with the "Polovtsian Dances" in the opera *Prince Igor* that they soon demanded a ballet group.

Michel Fokine, the great ballet revolutionist, made use of the English Morris Dance and the Polish Mazurka in his ballets. Leonide Massine followed with Spanish dances and Viennese Waltzes, Polkas, and the Can-can. Both David Lichine and George Balanchine employed character dance in their choreography. An abundance of ballets, operas, operettas, and musicals make use of the inheritance of national and character dances. They include *The Nutcracker, The Three-Cornered Hat, Rodeo, Carmen, Aida, The Bartered Bride, Fledermaus, Gypsy Baron, Oklahoma, Fiddler on the Roof,* and *West Side Story.*

Unfortunately, national and character dances are seldom incorporated in today's modern ballet presentations. Folk, character, and national dances are confined to groups specializing in only one type of technique, where they are used for presentations of individual dances rather than as vehicles for interpretation. The contemporary stage thrives on modern ballet technique, and at times it seems that the days of the story ballet, the simply expressed joy of dance, are lost. If one looks closely enough, however, national dance lives on in many modern creations, with steps surviving and frequently used in a style unrelated to their ethnic origin. There is a strong need for the revitalization of the instruction of this particular dance form, since it has such an important part to play in all dance productions.

In many parts of the world, dance companies with a character/national concept are growing and touring with much success, as well as preserving and developing their cultural inheritance and tradition. It is tragic that in the United States this field is almost entirely ignored. Dance is an elusive art. If we want it to continue, its forms must be handed down from master to pupil. Just as in the villages and courts of yesteryear, today's schools must continue this chain or the art of character dance will die of neglect.

Many students and dancers, seemingly ready to go "on the road," are unaware that character and national dance is an integral part of the well-rounded dancer's professional repertoire. At the Ballet Department of the Indiana University School of Music, where, as elsewhere, students arrive with little or no experience in this area, a character dance is always greatly welcomed and makes a good end to a working week. It is a "happy hour," stimulating to students and teacher alike and infectious in its feeling for the joy of dance.

A classically trained dancer will naturally adapt much more quickly than will dancers of other physical disciplines. Not all dancers are suited to this particular field. Achieving a brilliant technique requires special strength, stamina and perseverence, energy and vitality, and above all, joy—a short word meaning so much in all dance forms. Many, who by physique or temperament are not suited for a strictly classical dance career, can become demi-character dancers and will be able to devote themselves entirely to character work. Many fine classical dancers lack the artistry necessary for projecting and displaying emotion. This is never the case with the demi-character dancer, whose role demands this prerequisite.

Character dance can provide a valid and helpful change in the daily class. It will become, if properly taught, and with the right amount of enthusiasm, a lesson in which the students can cut loose and open up inner emotions. That will help them in projection, in developing their personal styles, and in stimulating more enthusiasm for their other dance studies. Technique, in and of itself, is merely a tool for the dancer and only the very basic requisite of the art. Character dance can ease the slow transition from technique to style, from inhibitions and shyness to outward projection.

Many persons are concerned about calf and thigh development in character work as well as in classical training. Physical therapists who have become involved in the art of dance believe that excessive development of the legs is usually the result of faulty or wrongly applied barre exercises over a period of time. However, muscle development depends to a large extent on the individual and is mostly inherited. Some dancers stay slim, no matter what they eat or what exercises they do, while others become bulky. To ensure proper development of the legs, the muscles should always be used to their fullest extent in both directions, so that a contraction is followed by a stretch. In addition, between movements of one leg or the other, the weight of the body must be placed equally on both feet for a moment, so that the muscle fiber relaxes.

As in classical ballet, every lesson begins with a series of exercises at the barre, to warm up the dancer's legs, arms, and body; to set the blood in circulation; and to gain balanced muscle tone. Exercises are designed to ensure correct placement and control of muscles and joints and to provide a firm foundation for progressive work in the center of the room. A proper warm-up prevents injury; it involves the right amount of exercise in a specific order. The teacher must differentiate between exercises for male and female dancers. Barres fixed to the walls around the classroom should be level with the elbow of the dancer of average height, approximately three and one-half feet from the floor. A second barre can be installed underneath for shorter students.

The proper attire for class is of great importance. The teacher must be able to see the line of the student's body in order to correct placement, and the dancer must be able to move freely as well as keep warm.

Male dancers should wear black nylon or wool tights, possibly with the addition of woolen leg warmers. A dance belt is of great importance, not only to give adequate support to the waist and abdomen but also for esthetic reasons. A T-shirt with short sleeves is recommended. Footwear for the male dancer demands special attention. Character shoes with one-half-inch to one-inch heels should be worn. They should fit well and be of professional quality. They should be laced or have elastic uppers similar to those on casual-wear slip-ons. Even better are character boots that come to just under the knee. They are certainly more expensive but well worth the price. No street shoes or street boots should be worn. At best, they give proper support for walking.

Female dancers should wear pink nylon tights, also with the possible addition of woolen leg warmers. A dance belt or girdle of soft flexible materials gives added support to the muscles of the lower body. The dance girdle is often neglected by women, but its importance cannot be stressed enough. It will not weaken the muscles, but rather supports them and helps prevent the spongy type of tissue that comes from overstretching the skin and the tissue below. The upper body should be clad in a leotard or blouse; and a knee-length skirt, cut on a full circle, completes the outfit. Hair should be a major concern for all dancers. Loose hair often obstructs the view of the dancer or her partner and so can lead to injury. Hair should be neatly pinned or secured by a ribbon, band, or "babushka." Long hair should be worn in a bun.

Throughout this book, in the directions for dance exercises and steps, the first column indicates the bars and (in italic) the beats of the music, the second describes the leg positions, and the third gives the arm and upper body positions.

The number of times an exercise is to be repeated is left to the discretion of the instructor, who should take into consideration the stamina and experience of the student.

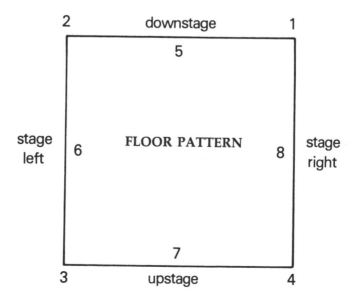

FOOT POSITIONS

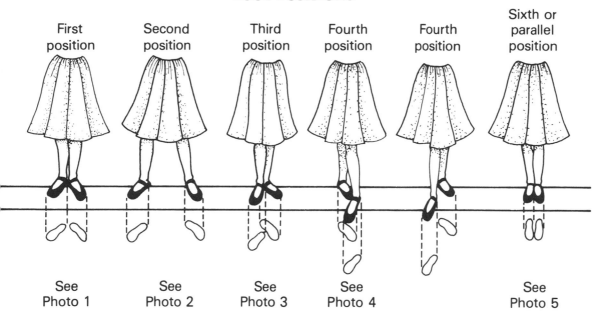

First position	Second position	Third position	Fourth position	Fourth position	Sixth or parallel position
See Photo 1	See Photo 2	See Photo 3	See Photo 4		See Photo 5

ARM POSITIONS

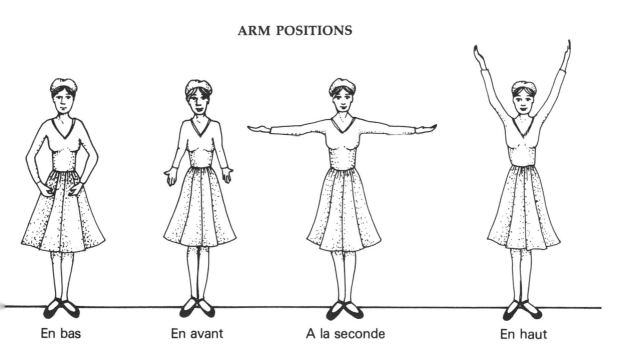

En bas   En avant   A la seconde   En haut

CHARACTER DANCE

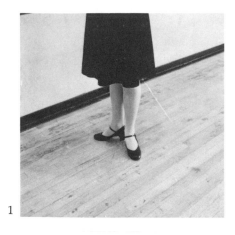

1

2

3

4

5

EXERCISES

Part One

1. Barre Exercises

Step 1. *Grand pliés* 2/4

3 chords*		Stand in 2nd position.	Place right hand on the barre, carry left arm from *en bas* over *en avant* to *à la seconde*, and with a reversed *port de bras*, finish with left hand on hip, fingers forward, thumb back (Photo 6).
Bars	1–2	Do a slow *grand plié* in 2nd position.	Move left arm to *à la seconde* and *en haut* (Photo 7), over barre side to *en bas*,
	3–4	Rise out of *grand plié*.	to *à la seconde*.

6

7

*All barre exercises begin with a three-chord preparation.

5	Do one quick *grand plié*.	Move left arm to *en bas*.
6	Rise out of *grand plié*.	Move left arm over *en bas* to *en avant* and to *à la seconde* (Photos 8, 9).
7	Lift both heels and beat *à terre* twice quickly (Photos 10, 11).	Reverse the *port de bras* back to hip position,
8	Stretch both knees.	elbows well forward.

Repeat exercise in 2nd position, then twice each in 1st, 4th, and 5th positions, *devant* and *derrière*.

Step 2. *Battements tendus* 2/4

3 chords		Stand in 3rd position, left foot in front.	Arm preparation as above.
Bars	1	Bring left leg to 4th position *en face, pointe tendue*.	Hold basic arm position throughout entire exercise.
	2	Lift the toes off the floor so that only the heel touches the floor (Photo 12). Bring supporting leg into *demi-plié* position.	
	3	Bring toes into *pointe tendue* position behind and stretch supporting leg.	
	4	Close left leg into 3rd position *demi-plié*.	

Repeat the leg movement *à la seconde, en arrière*, and *à la seconde* again. Then repeat the exercise with *demi-plié* on the supporting leg with the working leg in 4th position *en avant* with only the heel on the floor. Continue as before *en croix*.

Step 3.   2/4

| 3 chords | | Stand on right leg, left leg in *sur le cou-de-pied devant*. | Arm preparation as before. |
| | *and* | Do a *demi-plié* on supporting (right) leg, lift right heel off the floor. | Hold basic arm position throughout entire exercise. |

8

9

10

11

12

Bars	1	Bring left leg to *sur le cou-de-pied* behind right while doing one beat with right heel.	Shoulders show slight *épaulement*.
	2	Repeat, bringing left leg to *sur le cou-de-pied devant* (Photo 13).	
	3–8	Repeat three times.	
	9	Lift right heel off the floor and bring left leg to *seconde* with heel only touching the floor.	
	10	Beat once with right heel.	
	11	Bring left leg behind right into *coupé* position, tocs only resting on the floor, while right heel is lifted off the floor.	
	12	Beat once with right heel.	
	13	Open left leg to *seconde*, heel only touching the floor; lift right heel.	
	14	Beat once with right heel.	
	15	Bring left leg into *coupé* position in front of right leg, toes only resting on the floor, while right heel is lifted.	
	16	Beat once with right heel.	
	17–24	Repeat Step 3 *en croix* at twice the speed.	

Repeat all if desired.

Step 4. Mazurka 3/4 (Photos 14–16)

3 chords			Stand in 3rd position, right leg in front, left leg *sur le cou-de-pied derrière*.	Arm preparation as before.
Bars	1	1	Bring left leg to 4th position, *en avant* in *demi rond de jambe*, with only the toes touching the floor. At the same time, lift the right heel. Lower the right heel.	Bring left arm over *seconde* to *en avant*, with the back of the hand leading the movement.

13

14

15

16

	2	Lower the left heel in 4th position and lift the right heel again.	
	3	Lower the right heel and raise the left heel.	
2	*1*	Bring left leg in a *demi rond de jambe* over *à la seconde* to 4th position *en arrière* and place only the toes on the floor. At the same time, lift right heel. Lower the right heel.	Bring left arm, in a sweeping movement, over *à la seconde* to *en arrière*, elbow raised. Place the palm at the back of the neck. The head is inclined toward the right shoulder.
	2	Lower the left heel, and raise the right heel again.	
	3	Lower the right heel and raise the left heel.	
3–14		Repeat Step 4 seven times.	

Step 5. 3/4

3 chords		Stand with feet together in 6th position.	Arm preparation as before.
Bars	I	*1*	Do a "flic" with left leg, knee turned out *en arrière* of right leg.	Bring left arm over *demi en avant* to *à la seconde*, palm open.
		2	Turn in the left knee and do a	Bring left arm to *en avant*,
		3	"flic" *en dedans* of right leg *croisé devant*.	back of hand leading, then to *en bas*.
	2	*1*	Do a *développé en avant* with the left leg.	Bring left arm over *en avant* to *en haute* and *seconde*.
		2	Beat the floor once with the right heel (Photo 17).	
		3	Hold leg position.	
	3–4		Repeat above to *à la seconde*. Hold leg position.	Arm as before.
	5	*1*	Do a "flic" with turned-in knee *croisé devant* of right leg.	Bring left arm *en avant* and *en bas* with back of hand leading.

14

17

		2	Do a "flic" with turned-out knee	Move arms with palm open
		3	*en arrière* of supporting leg.	into *demi à la seconde*.
	6	1	*Battement développé en arrière* with the working leg.	Extend arm to rear in line with leg, palm down.
		2	Beat the floor with the heel of the supporting leg.	
		3	Hold leg position.	
	7–8		Repeat *à la seconde*.	Arm as before.
	9–16		Repeat Step 5 *en croix*.	

Step 6. 4/4

3 chords			Stand in 3rd position, left leg in front.	Arm preparation as before.
		and	Do a *grand battement* with left leg to *à la seconde* (Photo 18).	Move left arm to *en bas* and to *en haut*.
Bars	1	1	Place left leg in 2nd position on floor, foot turned out (Photo 19).	Move left arm to *à la seconde*, palm open.
		2	Lift left toes and turn on left heel so that toes are turned in (Photo 20).	Turn in palm, coming slowly to *en avant*.
		3	Lift left heel and turn on toes so that left heel approaches supporting leg (Photo 21). Raise toe and turn on heel so that toes are parallel to supporting foot.	Turn arm so that palm is open, continuing toward *en avant*. Turn arm so that palm is turned down.

15

18

19

20

21

	4		Stamp with left foot with full foot in 3rd position. Pause in above position.	Open arm to *demi en avant* with palm open.
	2–4		Repeat three times. Now reverse all and perform the following exercise four times:	
	and		Do a *grand battement à la seconde*.	Bring left arm over *en bas* to *à la seconde, en haut,* and back to *en bas*, palm down.
Bar	*1*	*1*	Bring left leg back into 3rd position, toes only touching the floor *en avant* of the right leg.	

16

	2	Turn left heel to the outside and place heel on floor.	Arm remains the same, and the head inclines toward the right shoulder;

3 Bring toes up and turn them to the outside.
Place the toes on the floor and bring up the heel again. Stamp in 2nd position.

move arm to *seconde* and gradually open palm.
Move to *à la seconde* and turn palm down.
Open palm in *seconde*.

4 Hold position.

Step 7. *2/4*

3 chords — Stand in 6th position facing the barre. *Demi-plié* on both legs. — Rest hands lightly on the barre.

Bars I   *1* Turn body slightly to left while lifting both heels (Photo 22). Turn heels to right side, keeping toes tightly together.

2 Place heels on the floor. Lift toes up and sideways (Photo 23), and place toes on the floor, while turning the body slightly to the right.

2–3 Repeat twice.

4 Stamp three times in 6th position, starting with left leg.

5–8 Repeat Step 7 to the other side.

9–16 Repeat both sequences.

22

23

Step 8.   *2/4*

3 chords			Stand in 1st position facing the barre. Do a *demi-plié* on both legs.

Rest hands lightly on the barre.

Bars	I	*1*	Simultaneously raise the left toes and the right heel and turn them so that the toes of both feet meet (Photos 24, 25).
		2	Now lift the left heel and the right toes, and turn both so that the two heels meet.
	2–3		Repeat twice.
	4		Stamp right, left, right, in 6th position.

24

25

26

5–8			Repeat all to other side.	
8–16			Repeat both sequences.	

Step 9. *2/4*

3 chords			Stand facing the barre in 3rd position, left foot in front, *demi-plié*.	Rest hands lightly on the barre.
Bars	1	*1*	With left leg do a *battement développé* to *à la seconde*, doing a slight hop on the right leg.	Hold body very loosely throughout the exercise; sway from the waist up from side to side.
		and	Bring left leg back to 3rd position *en avant* and lift right leg so that only the toes touch the floor (Photo 26).	
		2	Bring right heel down while lifting left heel.	
		and	Bring left heel down.	

Repeat Step 9 starting with right leg. Repeat entire exercise several times.

Step 10. *2/4*

3 chords			Face the barre standing in 6th position, *demi-plié*.	Rest both hands lightly on the barre.
Bars	1	*1*	Step with right foot *devant*, placing only heel on floor.	
		2	Place left heel next to right heel in 6th position (Photo 27).	
	2	*1*	Step onto 1/2 toe *en arrière* with right foot.	
		2	Bring left foot into same position next to right (Photo 28).	
	3	*1*	Step on right heel into *à la seconde* to the right.	
		2	Step on left heel into *à la seconde* to the left (Photo 29).	

27

28

29

4	*1*	Bring right leg back to original position.
	2	Bring left leg next to right in 6th position, slightly raised into 1/2 toe.

Repeat the exercise several times; repeat also at twice the speed. Reverse the exercise by stepping first into 1/2 toe.

Step 11. Prissjadka 2/4 (Boys only)

3 chords	Face the barre standing in 1st position.	Place both hands on the barre.

Bars	1		Do a *grand plié*, keeping heels together, knees open, heels lifted off the floor.
	2		Rise quickly, opening both legs into 2nd position standing on heels only.
	3–16		Repeat Step 11 seven times.
	17–24		This exercise should also be executed 4 times with both legs thrust *en l'air* and *en avant* while rising.
	25–32		Execute 4 times with both legs going to either left or right side *en l'air*.

Step 12. 2/4

3 chords			Stand in 2nd position.	Place right hand on the barre. Carry left arm from *en bas* over *en avant* to *en haut*.
Bars	1	1	Lift left leg from the knee as high as possible in *à la seconde* (*passé allongé*) (Photo 30).	
		2	Place left leg back on the floor in 2nd position.	
	2–4		Repeat three times.	

5	*1*	Repeat the above with a *demi-plié* on the supporting leg.	
	2	Stretch the knee of the supporting leg while placing the left leg back in 2nd position.	
6–8		Repeat three times.	
9		Repeat as above.	
10	*1*	Bring knee of working leg next to other knee, doing a *demi-plié* on both legs (Photo 31).	Bend the body toward the barre with the head almost touching the knee. Bring left arm down from *en haut* in front of the forehead.
	2	Straighten both legs in 6th position, facing the barre slightly.	
11	*1*	Lift left (working) leg into *à la seconde*, with knee bent upward, while doing a *demi-plié* on right leg.	Bring left arm to *en avant* and back again to *en haut*.
	2	Place left leg back into 2nd position *à terre* while straightening supporting leg.	
12	*1*	Do a *demi-plié* on the right leg while bringing the left leg into *sur le cou-de-pied* behind the right leg, the knee turned out (Photo 32).	Move left arm in a circle to the back of the head and place the palm on the neck. Open the body to the left, with left shoulder bent back and the head inclined to the left.
	2	Place working leg back into 6th position and straighten body.	Move left arm back into *en haut* position.
13–24		Repeat Step 12.	

Step 13.   4/4

3 chords	Stand in 3rd position, left leg in front.	Place right hand on barre, left hand on hip with fingers forward, thumb back.

22

31   32

Bars				
	I	*1*	Do a *grand battement* with left leg to *à la seconde;* hold left leg en *l'air* in *à la seconde*.	Move left arm in circle over *en haut* to *seconde*, palm open; left arm is in line with left leg, stretched to the rear.
		2	Do a *fouetté* so that the body is turned toward the barre (Photo 33). Face barre and do another lift of the leg from its *en l'air* position.	Left arm follows movements of left leg, palm leading and ending next to left leg and knee.
		3	Do a *grand plié* on the supporting (right) leg while the left leg, with knee turned in, brushes its instep over the floor and meets right foot in *grand plié* (Photo 34). (Both knees and heels together.)	
		4	Stand up quickly.	
	2	*1*	Open the left leg into a small *à la seconde* position.	Bring left arm into *en avant* position and right arm into *seconde*. Close arms in front of chest.
		2	Do a *pirouettes en dedans* on left leg, with right knee turned in.	Open arms *à la seconde*, palms open and *en avant*.
		3	Finish in small *seconde* position.	
		4	Close back into 3rd position.	
	3–8		Repeat Step 13 three times.	

23

33   34

Step 14.   *Tempo di Mazurka*   3/4

3 chords			Stand in 3rd position, left foot in front.	Arm preparation as before.
		and	Do a little hop on the right leg.	Face halfway toward the barre, turn head to left and look over left shoulder; keep left arm in hip position.
Bars	I	*1*	Bring the left foot to *demi à la seconde*, knee turned inward, toes only touching the floor, heel up (Photo 35).	
		2	Do another small hop on right leg while turning left leg out and opening it to *effacé devant*, heel touching the floor, toes up (Photo 36).	Turn body to *effacé*, opening left shoulder; open left arm to *seconde*, palm open.
		3	Do another small hop on the right leg, bringing the left leg *croisé devant* of right, toes only touching the floor (Photo 37).	With hand leading, left arm follows left leg across the lower body and aligns with left leg.
	2	*1*	Do a *fondu développé* into a *demi-seconde en l'air* with left leg.	Left arm opens to *seconde*, palm open; right arm leaves the barre.
		2	With right leg rise onto 1/2 toe.	
		3	Hold this position (Photo 38).	

24

35

36

37

38

3		Place left leg in small 2nd position.	
4	*1*	Do a *pirouette en dehors* on right leg.	Close arms in front of chest.
	2	Lift left leg behind supporting knee.	
	3	Finish in small 2nd position.	Open arms *à la seconde*, palms open, arms stretched slightly forward.
5–16		Repeat Step 14 three times. Less-advanced students should do the exercise at half speed.	

Step 15.   Grand battement   4/4

3 chords			Stand in 3rd position, left leg in front.	Arm preparation as above.
Bars	1	*1*	Do a *grand battement* with left leg to *en avant*, the right leg doing a *demi-plié* and one heel beat.	Left arm opens to *en haut* and then *seconde*, palm open.
			Lower working leg to *pointe tendue*, 4th position, *devant*.	Close left arm into hip position again, shoulder and elbow turned well forward.
		2	Do a "flic" with left toes over the floor and lift the leg to *passé* with knee slightly turned in.	
		3	Do a heel beat with right (supporting) leg.	
		4	Close left leg in 3rd position front.	
	2–8		Repeat Step 15 exercise to *à la seconde*, *en arrière*, *à la seconde* again, and *en croix* once more.	

Step 16.   Sur le cou-de-pied   3/4

3 chords			Stand on right leg, left leg in *sur le cou-de-pied devant*.	Arm preparation as before.
Bars	1	*1*	Lift and drop right heel while left foot is changing to *sur le cou-de-pied derrière* (Photo 39).	
		2	Beat right heel again while left leg is changing to front again (Photo 40).	
		3	Thrust left leg, as in a *frappé*, to *devant*, while sliding right leg forward in *demi-plié* (Photo 41).	Open left arm over *en haut* to *seconde*, palm open; head is inclined to left.
	2	*1*	Turning toward the barre, shift body weight onto left leg.	Grasp barre with left hand; move right hand from barre to hip position.
		2	Do a half turn so that the body faces in opposite direction.	

26

39

40

41

3	Bring right leg into *sur le cou-de-pied* position *devant*.
3–12	Repeat to other side, then repeat all of Step 16 four times.

This exercise may also be executed thrusting the leg into *à la seconde*, then doing a "flic-flac" movement behind the supporting leg and a turn *en dehors*, then changing legs. Arms go to *en haut* during the turn.

2. *Center Exercises*

POLKA STEPS

Step 1. 2/4

			Stand in 3rd position, right leg in front.	Hold right arm with fist *en avant*, left arm behind body at same level, or both arms in hip position.
		and	Hop on left leg.	
Bars	I	*1*	*Do a skip like a chassé*, stepping on right to *effacé devant*.	(Photo 42, with arms in hip position.)
		and	Bring left leg behind right leg.	
		2	Open right left to *effacé devant* into 4th position.	
		and	Open left leg, passing the right leg.	Reverse arms.
	2	*1*	Step on left leg into 4th position *effacé devant*.	
		and	Bring right leg behind left leg.	
		2	Open left leg again to *effacé devant*.	

This step can also be done to one side only or with a turn, like a "hopped" *chaîné*.

Step 2. *Counterclockwise step* 2/4

			Stand in 6th position.	Arms in hip position.
Bars	I	*1*	Step slightly sideways on right leg.	

42   43

		Step with left leg *croisé devant* over right.
2	*1*	Step on right leg into small *à la seconde*.
	2	Close left leg to right.
3	*1*	Hop on left leg, bringing right leg into 4th position *croisé devant*, touching the floor once with the toes (Photo 43).
	2	Bring right leg to *effacé devant*, touching the floor.
4	*1*	Bring right leg to 6th position, raising both legs to 6th position, 1/2 toe.
	2	Lower and rise, lower and rise, very fast in 6th position.

Step 3. German Polka 2/4

			Stand in 6th position.	Arms in hip position.
		and	Hop on left leg.	
Bars	I	*1*	Place right heel *en avant* (Photo 44).	Left shoulder *épaulement*.
		and	Hop on left leg.	
		2	Place right toes slightly *en arrière* (Photo 45).	Right shoulder *épaulement*.
		and	Hop on left leg.	

29

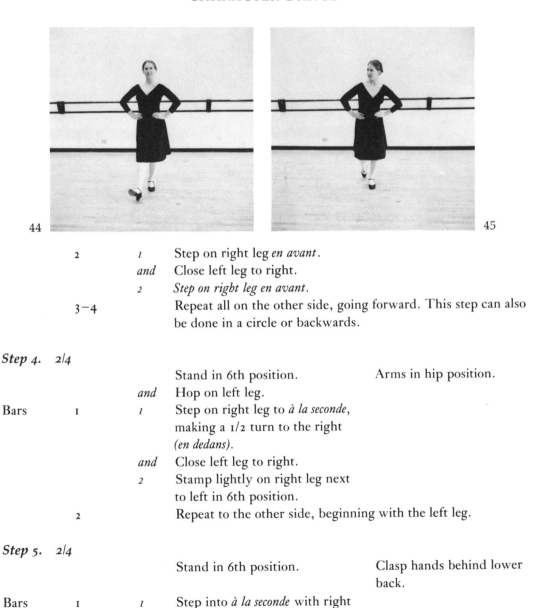

44   45

2	*1*	Step on right leg *en avant*.
	and	Close left leg to right.
	2	*Step on right leg en avant.*
	3–4	Repeat all on the other side, going forward. This step can also be done in a circle or backwards.

Step 4. 2/4

			Stand in 6th position.	Arms in hip position.
		and	Hop on left leg.	
Bars	I	*1*	Step on right leg to *à la seconde*, making a 1/2 turn to the right (*en dedans*).	
		and	Close left leg to right.	
		2	Stamp lightly on right leg next to left in 6th position.	
	2		Repeat to the other side, beginning with the left leg.	

Step 5. 2/4

			Stand in 6th position.	Clasp hands behind lower back.
Bars	I	*1*	Step into *à la seconde* with right leg and do a *demi-plié*.	
		and	Bring left leg behind right with toes only touching the floor.	
		2	Hop once on right leg in *sur le cou-de-pied* position.	
	2–4		Repeat Step 5 to other side, then to each side with 1/2 turn.	

30

Step 6. 2/4

			Stand in 6th position, *demi-plié.*	Arms in hip position.
		and	Jump off both feet.	
Bars	1	*1*	Beat heels together *(cabriole).*	
		and	Land on both legs in 6th position, *demi-plié.*	
		2	Rise in 6th position and come back to *demi-plié.*	
	2—4		Repeat Step 6 three times.	

RUSSIAN STEPS

Step 1. Kazanski pas de basque 2/4

			Stand in 1st position	Boys put hands on lapels of vest. Girls put hands on hips.
Bars	1	*1*	Do a *pas de basque* with knees lifted very high *en avant*, moving slightly right and left: Lift right leg with knee bent up very high *en avant*. Place right leg in small turned-in 2nd position, while raising knee high *en avant*.	Arms can be opened to *à la seconde.*
		and	Place left leg down next to right and raise right leg high.	
		2	Place right leg next to left leg.	Close arms in hip position.
	2		Repeat Step 1 to other side.	

Step 2. 2/4

			Stand in 1st position.	Boys fold arms across chest. Girls put hands on hips.
Bars	1	*1*	Hop on left leg, bringing right knee *en avant*, very high (Photo 46).	Lift left arm to *en haut* and slap right knee with right hand.
		2	Repeat hop on left leg.	Slap right knee again.

31

46

2	1	Hop on right leg, bringing left knee *en avant*, very high.	Reverse arms and slap left knee.
	2	Repeat hop on right leg.	Slap left knee again.
3	1	Hop on left leg, bringing right knee *en avant*, very high.	Lift left arm *en haut* and slap right knee with right hand.
	2	Hop onto right leg, bringing left knee high, *en avant*.	Lift right arm *en haut* and slap left knee with left hand.
4		Repeat bar 3 bringing left knee high, *en avant*, then right knee.	
5–6		Repeat Bars 1 and 2.	
7		Repeat Bar 4.	
8		Stamp right, left, right, in 6th position.	Open the arms parallel, palms open, *en avant*.

Step 3. **Trepak (Pas marché with accent on 1st step)** 2/4

Bars			Stand in 1st position.	Fold arms across chest.
	1	1	Step with left leg *en avant*, brushing right leg briskly past left to *effacé devant*.	Open both arms to *à la seconde*, palms open.
		and	Place right leg on floor.	
		2	Place left leg on floor.	
	2	1	Stamp on right leg, brushing left leg briskly past right to *effacé devant*.	Bring both arms over *en avant* back to hip position.

and	Place left leg on floor.
2	Place right leg on floor.

Step 4.   Russian Cabrioles.   Usually 2/4

Fold arms across chest.

a.
Jump off the floor, bringing
right leg in a *grand battement
effacé devant* while folding left
leg under the body in a *passé*.

During the jump open one
arm to *en haut*.

b. Bell-shaped cabriole
Jump off the floor with both
legs, bringing right leg into a
grand battement effacé devant,
then bring feet together so that
the toes touch.

Fold arms across chest.

BELL-SHAPED CABRIOLE

Step 5. 2/4

| | | | Stand in 1st position, *demi-plié*. | Boys fold arms across chest. Girls hold hands in hip position with elbows turned well forward. |

Bars	1	*1*	Hop on left leg, lift right knee *devant*, and place right heel on the floor.
		and	Hop on left leg again.
		2	Bring right leg *en arrière* with toes only touching the floor.
	2	*1*	Hop on left leg, placing full right foot *devant*.
		and	Step on left leg. Step on right leg (running steps).

Step 6. *Gormoshka ("The Harmonica")* 2/4

| | | | Stand in 1st position. | Arms in hip position. |
| | | *and* | Hop off left leg while the right leg is lifted into a "turned-in" *passé*, the foot resting briefly on the side of the left knee (Photos 47, 48). | Bring left arm to *en avant*, right arm to *à la seconde*, both hands forming fists. At the same time bend the body over the left leg *cambré*. |

Bars	1	*1*	Bring right leg next to left foot, and just before touching the floor, open right leg to a small *à la seconde* position, with only the heel touching the floor, toes well up and turned out (Photo 49).	Swing the arms over *en bas* to the left *à la seconde*.
		and	Lift left leg with bent knee.	
		2	Step with left foot close to right leg.	Bring arms to *en bas* position.
		and	Hop off left leg.	Arms as at beginning of step.
	2		Repeat toward right side.	
	3–4		Repeat Bars 1 and 2.	
	5		Stamp right, left, right.	
	6–10		Repeat all of Step 6 to other side.	

34

47

48

49

Step 7.   *Podshechka (Russian mill or "coffee grinder")   2/4 (Boys only)*

			Stoop in 1st position *grand plié*, 1/2 toe, and extend left leg into *à la seconde*.	Lean forward and place both hands on the floor to support the body.
Bars	I	*1*	Bring left leg in a *rond de jambe à terre* to *en avant*, to *croisé devant*, and continue toward right side.	Lift each arm off the floor briefly to let the leg pass.
		and	Continue the circle with the left leg and lift the right leg, in its *grand plié* position, to let the left leg pass, then place the right leg back on floor.	Lean well forward to enable the right leg to be lifted.

35

		2	Continue the circle with the left (working) leg until it is again in *à la seconde* on the left side. Repeat Step 7 several times.	

Step 8. *Russki Schag* 2/4 *(Girls only)*

			Stand in 1st position.	Arms in hip position.
Bars	1	*1*	Step *devant* onto 1/2 toe with right foot.	Open arms *à la seconde*.
		and	Step *devant* onto 1/2 toe with left foot.	
		2	Step *devant* onto 1/2 toe with right foot.	
		and	Lift left foot slightly off the floor and bring it *en avant*.	
	2		Repeat Step 8.	Close arms in hip position.

Step 9. *Bokowoi Schag ("Sidestep")* 2/4

			Stand in 1st position.	Arms in hip position.
Bars	1	*1*	Step softly with right foot onto 1/2 toe.	
		2	Bring left leg onto 1/2 toe near right heel.	
		and	Lift right leg off floor sharply. Repeat Step 9. This movement is often used when turning in place.	

Step 10. 2/4

			Stand in 3rd position, right foot in front.	Arms in hip position or folded across chest.
Bars	1	*1*	Step with right leg to 4th position *effacé devant*, placing only heel on the floor, toes well lifted.	Open arms to *seconde*, palm up, left shoulder forward.
		and	Place left foot onto 1/2 toe behind right heel.	
		2	Step slightly *en avant* on full right foot.	Close arms over *en avant* to hip position.
	2		Repeat Step 10 starting with left leg.	

36

Step 11. **2/4 (Each step is done with a 1/2 turn.)**

			Stand in 3rd position, right foot in front.	Arms in hip position.
Bars	1	*1*	Step *en avant* with right knee slightly bent into small 4th position.	
		and	Bring left leg *sur le cou-de-pied en arrière* of right in *coupé*, touching the floor with toes once.	
		2	Hop on right leg in *demi-plié*.	
		and	Left toes touch the floor *en arrière* once, in a very quick movement!	
	2	*1*	Make a 1/2 turn to the right and place left leg *croisé devant* of the right.	Lower right arm, back of hand lifted and pointing toward the floor at same angle as the body.
		and	Right toes touch floor, once *en arrière*.	
		2	Hop on left leg in small *demi-plié*.	
		and	Right toes touch floor once *en arrière*.	Lift left arm with elbow bent and back of hand cupped up.

Step 12. **2/4**

			Stand in 1st position	Arms in hip position.
Bars	1	*1*	Jump into 2nd position, toes turned in and on 1/2 toe.	
		and	Jump again and bring feet together.	Open arms in *demi-seconde*, palms open.
		2	Place left leg *en arrière* of right calf, as in *jeté*.	
		and	Jump as before	Hold arms *en avant*, as in usual *pirouettes*.
	2	*1*	into 2nd position.	
		and	Do a 1/2 turn to the right	
		2	into 3rd position, 1/2 toe, left leg in front.	

CHARACTER DANCE

Step 13.   *Cobbler's step*   *2/4 (Boys only)*

			Stand in 1st position.	Cross arms over chest.
Bars	1	*1*	Go into *grand plié* in 1st position.	
		and	Hop in slightly risen position on right leg.	Open arms to *seconde*.
		2	Bring left leg *croisé en avant* of right with bent knee, still remaining in *grand plié*.	Slap left foot with right hand; hold left hand *en haut*.
		and	Go back into deepest *plié* in 1st position.	
	2		Repeat Step 13 with other leg and arms reversed.	

HUNGARIAN STEPS

Step 1.   *Csárdás*   *2/4*

			Stand in 1st position.	Arms in hip position.
		and	Skip back slightly on right leg.	
Bars	1	*1*	Lift left foot to right calf, turned out a little, and step *croisé devant* over right leg (Photo 50).	Bring arms *en avant* with palms open in an offering gesture.
		and	Skip back slightly on left leg.	
		2	Bring right leg *croisé devant*, a little turned out, over left leg (Photo 51).	

50 51

2–8   The complete movement goes forward or back or *en diagonale* with 1/2 turns *à la chaîné*. Going backward the arms move over *seconde* to *en avant* and back into hip position.

Step 2. *Standard Hungarian finishing steps*   4|4

			Stand in 1st position.	Arms *à la seconde*, palms up.
		and	Hop lightly on left leg while the right does a *frappé* movement *effacé devant*.	Start bending forward from the waist.
Bars	1	*1*	Place right leg, toes turned in, *croisé devant* of left, both legs in *demi-plié* (Photo 52).	Lean well forward and bend to left side, with left arm *en avant*, right remaining *à la seconde*.
		2	With a little jump open both legs into a *à la seconde* position, knees bent, toes turned in and in 1/2 toe position (Photo 53).	Open left arm back to *seconde*, pull head down with chin to chest; the hands are "broken" at the wrists and turned out.
		3	Bring legs together in 1st position in 1/2 toe, clicking heels together (Photo 54).	Straighten body, turn arms so that palms are open.
		4	Stand still.	
	2–4		Repeat Step 2 to the other side, then repeat both sides with 1/2 turns.	

Step 3. *Bokazo ("Heel click")*   2|4

			Stand in 1st position.	Arms are *à la seconde*.
		and	Rise on left leg onto 1/2 toe while raising right knee. Keep right toes turned in, so that the heel is the highest point of the right foot. The knees are almost together (Photo 55).	Turn arms in *à la seconde* so that palms are down and toward the back.
Bars	1	*1*	Bring heels sharply together in 1/2 toe position.	Turn arms around so that the palms are open.
		and	Rise on right leg onto 1/2 toe while raising left knee. Keep left toes turned in, so that left heel is the highest point of the foot. The knees are almost together.	Arms as above.

39

52

53

54

55

2	Bring heels together sharply in 1st position 1/2 toe.

Step 4.   2/4

			Stand in 1st position.	Arms in hip position.
Bars	I	*1*	Jump from left leg onto right leg, lifting the knee very high but holding it close to the right leg.	Open arms over *en avant* and *en haut* to *seconde*, leaning the body to the right and inclining the head.
		and	Lift left leg in same fashion and place left foot next to right on floor (Photo 56).	

56   57

	2	Stamp once on right foot, then lift right foot lightly off the floor.	Close arms over *en haut* and *en avant* to hip position.
	2	Repeat Step 4 to other side, reversing body movement.	

Step 5.   *2/4*

			Stand in 1st position.	Arms in hip position.
Bars	1	*1*	Slide the right leg, stretched to *à la seconde demi-en l'air*, while doing a *demi-plié* on the left leg (Photo 57).	Move both arms in a swinging movement over *en bas* to right side *à la seconde*, body leaning to left side.
		and	Bring right leg next to the left in 6th position, 1/2 toe.	Bring arms to *en bas*.
		2	Stamp once lightly with left foot next to right.	Straighten body.
	2–16		Repeat Step 5 three times to the right, four times to the left, then four times each to the right and left with 1/2 turns.	

Step 6.   *4/4*

			Stand in 1st position.	Arms are *à la seconde*, palms open.
Bars	1	*1*	Jump from both legs and land on left leg in *demi-plié;* the right leg, with bent knee, lifted to *croisé devant* (Photo 58).	Slap the right heel in *croisé* with left hand; the right arm is *en haut*.

41

58

59

60

61

62

		2	Move lower part of right leg to *seconde* while the knee stays turned in, so that the right heel is the highest point of the foot in *à la seconde* (Photo 59).	Slap the right heel with the right hand; the left arm is *en haut*.
		3	With knees held together, bring right leg to *croisé en arrière* of left leg (Photo 60).	Slap the right heel with left hand; the right arm is *en haut*.
		4	Hop into 6th position.	Arms in *à la seconde*, palms open.
	2		Repeat Step 6 to other side.	

Step 7. 4/4

			Stand in 1st position.	Arms in hip position.
Bars	1	*1*	Step with left leg to 4th position *croisé devant*.	
		2	Do a slight skip on left leg while opening the right leg *effacé devant* in a very high *développé*.	Open left arm to *en haut* position, with the head inclined to the open arm, left shoulder *épaulé* (right arm remains in hip position).
		3	Step briefly onto left knee, with right leg in 4th position *effacé devant*, and draw left foot to right into 6th position *grand plié*.	Bring left arm far back to *à la seconde*, then to *en bas* next to left foot.
		4	Stand up facing *effacé* toward stage location 1 (Photo 61).	Open left arm in *seconde*, palm open, and place right hand, with well turned-out elbow, behind head.
	2	*1*	Push from left leg onto right leg, bringing it into 2nd position, *demi-plié*, but turned in. The left leg remains in *demi-en l'air* and stretched (Photo 62).	With left arm outstretched, turn hand so palm is down.
		2	Bring left foot to right in 1/2 toe position and repeat, pushing off left leg onto right leg into 2nd position *demi-plié*.	Open right arm.

43

	3	Step with left leg over right *croisé devant* 4th position and bring right heel to *seconde en l'air* (not very high). The right knee stays turned in.	Cross wrists, low, in front of body, palms down. Open arms, low, *à la seconde*, with "broken" wrists and palms down.
	4	Snap heels together in demi-1/2 toe (bokazo).	Turn palms up, hands outstretched.

Step 8. 4/4

			Stand in 1st position, turning body toward stage location 2.	Arms *à la seconde*, palms open.
Bars	I	*1*	Step with right leg over left *croisé devant* (small 4th position) and raise left leg with turned-in knee to *sur le cou-de-pied*.	Bring left arm *en avant* and stretch right arm to *effacé en arrière*.
		2	Thrust left leg as in a *frappé* to *effacé devant*, passing the right foot through 6th position; then bring left leg in similar movement back in front of right leg (Photo 63).	Arms remain in same position.
		3	Turn body to face 1 and thrust the left leg in *frappé* to *croisé devant* (Photos 64, 65).	Right arm goes into *en avant* in front of chest; left arm is stretched out *effacé en arrière*.

Immediately bring the foot back in *frappé*, passing parallel to the

63

64

65

right foot, through 6th position, and end in *coupé* position behind right (supporting) leg, left knee turned out and *demi-plié*.

4   Turn to face 5, and with a sharp movement, bring left leg, slightly turned out, to 1st position next to right.   Open arms into *à la seconde*, palms down, then open palms.

Step 9. *Csárdás-friss ("fast")* 2/4

			Stand in 6th position	Arms in hip position.
Bars	1	1	Stamp with full right foot sideways to *à la seconde*.	Open arms in *seconde*, palms open, with left shoulder *épaulement* and head inclined to the right.
		and	Bring left full foot next to right in 6th position.	
		2	Step again with right leg, parallel to left into 2nd position.	
		and	Bring left foot back into 6th position next to right, now on 1/2 toe with a special strong stamp.	
	2		Repeat to left side, starting with left leg. Reverse arm and body movements.	
	3	1	Stamp with right leg, lifting left leg slightly off the floor.	Arms *à la seconde*.

	and	Stamp with left leg, lifting right leg slightly off the floor.	
	2	Repeat above right, left,	
	and	right, in very fast movement, with knees close to each other in 6th position.	
4	*1*	Make a small jump with both feet in 6th position (Photo 66, but with right arm in front), turning body to face 2.	Bring left arm to *en avant* across chest and right arm *effacé en arrière*, stretched out.
	and	Repeat, turning body to face 1.	Reverse arms.
	2	Repeat, turning body to face 2.	Reverse arms.

66

67

Step 10.   Dobanto ("Drumming step")   2/4

		Stand in 3rd position, right foot in front.	Arms in hip position.
	and	Do a small *sauté* onto the left foot, raising right leg sur *le cou-de-pied devant*.	Bring right arm *en avant*, crossing the chest; bring left arm behind the back.
Bars	I	*1*	Stamp with right leg slightly *croisé devant* of left, at the same time lifting the left leg *sur le cou-de-pied en arrière*.	
		2	Stamp on left leg *croisé derrière* of right, lifting right leg *devant* in *sur le cou-de-pied*.	

2–32   Repeat Step 10 seven times to the right, eight times to the left, then eight times each with turns *tombé* and *sur le cou-de-pied*.

Step 11. Lejto (Cabriole with outstretched legs) 2/4

	Stand in 6th position.	Hold left arm *en haut* and right arm in hip position.
and	Do a small *sauté*, stretching the right leg, toes lifted, and bringing the left leg slightly *seconde*, also stretched; beat heels together; and land in *demi-plié* on right leg.	

Bars   1   *1*   Stamp on left leg.

                    2   Stamp on right leg in 6th position.

2–16   The cabriole can be done with the right or the left leg, also in turns to the right or left. If the cabriole is done with bent knees it is called Bokavero.

Step 12. Cou-de-talon 2/4

	Stand in 6th position.	
and	Step with left leg *croisé devant* over right leg (small 4th position) (Photo 67).	Bend body forward and toward location 2, left arm crossed over chest *en avant* and over right arm, which is slightly lower and crosses over body to opposite side. Incline head to left shoulder.

Bars   1   Brush out the right leg to *à la seconde, demi-en l'air*, with turned-in foot, sliding sideways on left foot at the same time (Photo 68).   Open both arms to *seconde*; turn head to right in the direction of the executed movement.

                2   Bring right leg to left leg into *demi-plié* and 6th position at the end of the slide (Photo 69). There is *no* beat!   Bring arms back and across body *en avant* in opposite direction.

Repeat Step 12 several times to one side, then the other.

47

68   69

YUGOSLAV STEPS

Step 1. *3/8*

		Stand in 6th position.	Arms in hip position.
Bars	1	Hop with feet in 6th position.	
	2	Hop with feet in 6th position.	
	3	Hop, landing only on left leg, while right foot is lifted to calf.	
	4	Hop on right leg, lifting left foot to calf.	
	5–16	Repeat Step 1 three times; end third repeat by stamping left, right, left, right.	

When this step is done by partners, boy and girl each hold their arms criss-crossed. The boy lets the girl pass in front of him, holding her hands, or turns her under his arms or around himself.

Step 2. *3/8*

		Stand in 6th position.	Arms in hip position.
Bars	1	Hop on left leg, while right leg touches the floor, *pointe tendue efface devant.*	Turn body slightly in the direction of the moving leg (*épaulement*).

48

2	Bring right leg to *croisé devant*, touching the floor *pointe tendue* in front of left leg.	

3	Bend right leg and bring right foot behind left in *sur le cou-de-pied*, touching the floor.
4	Close feet in 6th position.
5–8	Repeat Step 2 to other side.

Step 3. 3/8 (Boys only)

		Stand in 6th position.	Arms *à la seconde*, palms up.
Bars	1	Go into *grand plié* with knees held tightly together.	
	2–3	Rise, turning knees to right and left, feet in 1/2 toe position.	Move body in same direction as legs.
	4	Repeat movement rising.	

The knee movement can also be done while going into the *grand plié*.

Step 4. 3/8

		Stand in 6th position.	Arms in hip position, with a handkerchief in the right hand.
Bars	1	Jump lightly on right leg while the left is brought *devant* and lifted off the floor.	Twirl handkerchief and wave it while doing the step.
	2	Place left leg on floor with a slight jump, while right leg is brought *en avant* and stretched *pointe tendue*.	
	3	Repeat with other leg.	
	4	Place left leg *devant*, heel only touching the floor, toes up.	
	5–8	Repeat Step 4 to other side, starting with other leg. The movement is very fast.	

CHARACTER DANCE

Step 5. *3/8*

		Stand in 3rd position, right leg in front.	Arms in hip position.
Bars	1	Stamp with right heel in 4th position *en avant*.	
	2	Repeat.	
	3	Repeat.	
	4	Place right leg behind left.	Turn left shoulder forward.
	5	Place left leg in 2nd position.	
	6	Place right leg in front of left leg.	
	7	Turn on right leg *en dedans*.	
	8	Lift left leg into very high turned-in *passé croisé devant*.	
	9–16	Repeat Step 5 to other side.	

Step 6. *3/8*

		Stand in 3rd position, right leg in front.	Arms in hip position.
Bars	1	Brush right foot with full sole *croisé devant* of left leg.	
	2	Repeat behind.	
	3	Repeat in front.	
	4	Close right leg to left, 6th position.	
	5	Brush left foot with full sole *croisé devant* of right leg.	
	6	*Tombé* onto left leg, right leg *coupé derrière* in *sur le cou-de-pied*.	
	7	Step on right leg behind left.	
	8	Close left leg to right in 6th position.	

Step 7. *Sedam ("Seven")* *2/4*

			Stand in 1st position.	Arms in hip position.
Bar	1	1	Step with right leg to *à la seconde*.	
		2	Close left leg behind in 3rd position.	

50

	2	*1*	Repeat with right leg *seconde*.	
		2	Repeat, closing left behind.	
	3	*1*	Repeat with right leg.	
		2	Repeat with left leg.	
	4	*1*	Repeat with right leg.	
		2	Remain in 2nd position.	
	5–8		Repeat Step 7 to other side.	

Step 8. 2/4

			Stand in 3rd position, right leg in front.	Arms in hip position.
Bars	1	*1*	Step with right leg to *à la seconde*.	
		2	Close left leg to right in 6th position.	
	2	*1*	Step with right to *seconde* and hop on right leg, bringing left leg in *demi passé* turned-in *devant*.	
		2	Step on left foot.	
	3	*1*	Hop on left foot, bringing right leg *croisé devant* in an open *coupé*.	
		2	Step on right leg behind left.	
	4	*1*	Do a *frappé-ballonné*-like movement with left leg *croisé devant* of right.	
		2	Hop once on right leg.	
	5–8		Repeat Step 8 to other side.	

TARANTELLA STEPS   6/8

Step 1.

Introduction, 2 beats.		Stand in 3rd position, right foot in front.	Arms *en haut*, holding a tambourine, throughout.
Bars	1	Do a *petit pas de basque* with slightly bent knees to the right side: Step onto right foot, 1/2 toe, with slight *sauté;*	

immediately bring the left leg *croisé devant* into small 4th position over right in *demi-plié*. Hop with right foot to the side again onto 1/2 toe and bring left leg *croisé en arrière* into small 4th position behind right leg. (The knees stay in *demi-plié* throughout the *sautés* and crossings, and the feet always land in 1/2 toe position.)

Repeat Step 1 several times to one side and then to the other.

Step 2.

	Stand in 4th position, right foot in front.	Hold tambourine in left hand in hip position; support by holding rim with right hand.
Bars	1	Jump to the right in the manner of a *grand jeté en tournant*, swinging the left leg in a semicircle to the right side; left leg lands in *demi-plié devant*; right knee is on floor *en arrière*.	Move left arm to *à la seconde* and beat tambourine on floor with right hand at time of landing.
	2	Remain in same position.	Beat tambourine on left knee.
	3	Remain in same position.	Beat tambourine on right elbow.
	4	Stand up in 6th position.	Bring left hand *en haut* to beat tambourine.
	5	*Relevé* onto 1/2 toe in 6th position, then lower heels.	Open arms into *à la seconde*, tambourine in right hand.
	6–8	Repeat bar 5 three times.	

Repeat all of Step 2 several times.

Step 3.

	Stand in 1st position.	Hold tambourine over head with both hands.

Bars	1–2	Hop lightly onto right leg, simultaneously thrusting left leg in *frappé* or *ballonné* to *croisé devant*. Do another *sauté* and hop with a *frappé* using the same legs.	
	3–4	*Sauté* lightly *à la seconde* with left leg while right does a *frappé croisé devant* of left. *Sauté* lightly on left and do a *frappé croisé devant* with the right.	

Repeat Step 3 several times in each direction as well as backwards.

Step 4.

		Stand in 3rd position, right foot in front.	Left arm in hip position; hold tambourine in right hand at left side of waist.
Bars	1	Do a *chassé* with right leg toward stage location 8 in *arabesque demi-plié*.	Slowly extend right arm in the direction of the *chassé*, tambourine *devant*.
	2	*Sauté* in *demi-plié* toward 8.	
	3–6	Repeat *sauté* or *temps levé* 4 times.	
	7	Slide left leg *in failli* toward 8.	
	8	Do a *contretemps* with right leg to the left, changing direction toward 6.	Change hands on tambourine and bring left arm *devant* toward 6.
	9–16	Repeat Step 4 starting toward location 6 and ending toward 8.	

Step 5.

		Stand in 1st position.	Hold tambourine on hip with left hand; support with right hand.
Bars	1	Go onto left knee, right foot in *effacé devant*.	Beat tambourine with left hand on floor in front, right arm *en haut*.
	2	Remain in kneeling position.	Beat tambourine on right knee.

	3	Remain in kneeling position.	Beat tambourine on right elbow.
	4	Remain in kneeling position.	Beat tambourine with right hand.
	5–8	Remain in kneeling position.	Bring tambourine in semicircle over *à la seconde*, shaking it; move right arm correspondingly.
	9–11	Repeat bars 1–3.	
	12	Stand up.	Beat tambourine with right hand.
	13–16	Rise, then lower onto heel from 1/2 toe position.	Bring tambourine in semicircle *à la seconde*.

Step 6. Circle movement to the right

		Stand in 3rd position, right foot in front.	Hold tambourine on hip with left hand; support with right hand.
Bars	1	Step on right leg into *demi-plié effacé devant*.	Move arms to *en avant*.
	2	Do a *grand battement en cloche* with left leg *en avant* (in direction of circle) and do a *temps levé*.	Beat the tambourine in *en avant* position at waist level.
	3	Step on left leg in direction of circle *en avant*, *demi-plié*.	Open arms over *seconde*.
	4	Do a *grand battement en cloche (en arrière)*, brushing right leg back, and do a *temps levé* on left leg.	Beat tambourine with both hands behind the back.
	5–8	Take four running steps *(à la jeté)*, starting with right leg.	Bring tambourine and arms back to hip position.
		Repeat several times.	

Step 7. Fouetté turn

		Stand on right leg and place left leg *sur le cou-de-pied* back.	Hold tambourine on hip with left hand; support with right hand.
Bars	1	Do a *coupé* on left leg *en arrière*, immediately bringing the right leg over *demi en l'air* to *seconde*,	With right arm bring tambourine *en haut* and slightly behind the head.

54

2	to *croisé en arrière* of left leg, and turn body over *en dehors* to a small 4th position, right leg *en avant*.	Bring tambourine *en avant* and beat it with left hand.
3–16	Repeat Step 7 three times, then four times to the other side (a *renversé* movement).	

Step 8. Soutenu en tournant

	Stand in 3rd position, right foot in front.	Hold tambourine on hip with left hand; support with right hand.
Bars	1	Do a *demi-plié*, *sauté* with right leg onto right 1/2 toe; immediately bring left leg with a *rond de jambe demi en l'air* to *croisé devant* over right leg onto 1/2 toe.	
	2	Turn on both legs on 1/2 toe, *en dedans;* at the completion of the turn the right leg is in 4th position *devant*.	Lift arms *en haut* and beat tambourine over the head; then open arms to *à la seconde*.
	3–8	Repeat Step 8 three times to the same side. This step is often called *petit* or *grand pas de basque en tournant*, depending on how high the *sauté* and *grand battement* to *à la seconde* are executed.	

Step 9.

	Stand in 6th position.	Hold tambourine in left hand at left hip; support with right hand.
Bars	1	Do a small *sauté* on both legs in 6th position.	Beat the tamborine in *en avant* position.
	2	Do a *grand battement* with right leg while doing a small *sauté* on the left.	Beat the tamborine with both hands under the knee of lifted leg.
	3–4	Repeat Step 9 with other leg. Repeat both movements several times.	

CHARACTER DANCE

Step 10. *Moving from left to right*

	Stand in 6th position.	Hold the tambourine with both hands behind the back.
Bars 1	Do a *sauté* on left leg, bringing right leg to *à la seconde* slightly turned in, 1/2 toe.	Arms remain behind the back.
2	Do another *sauté* on left leg, leaving right in *seconde*, heel only touching the ground and toes slightly turned out.	Incline the head and turn it to the right and left.

Repeat several times on both sides.

MAZURKA STEPS   3/4 or 3/8

Step 1.

		Stand in 3rd position, right foot in front.	Hands in hip position.
Bars 1	1	Do a *tombé-chassé* with right leg slightly *effacé devant* into *arabesque demi-plié*.	Open right arm to *en avant* and to *à la seconde*, palm open (Photo 70).
	2	Do a *temps levé* in *demi-plié*.	
	3	Brush left leg past right in a *ballonné devant* and finish with left leg in *sur le cou-de-pied* in front of right (Photo 71).	Bring right arm back into hip position.
	2	Repeat Step 1 with left leg.	

Step 2.

		Stand in 3rd position, right foot in front.	Arms in hip position.
Bars 1	1	Stamp with right foot into 4th position *devant* (Photo 72).	Open right arm over *en avant* to *à la seconde*, palm open.
	2	Step with left leg into 3rd position behind right.	

70

71

72

3	Do a *ballonné* with right leg slightly *effacé devant* and bring right leg back to *sur le cou-de-pied devant* of left (as in Photo 71). Repeat several times.	Bring right arm, palm down, over *en avant*, across the body at waistline, to left hand.

Step 3.

			Stand in 1st position.	Arms in hip position.
Bars	I	*I*	Bring right leg into a small *à la seconde*, beat with left leg—jumping off the ground—in 6th position, heels clicking and toes slightly lifted.	Open arms *à la seconde*, palms open.

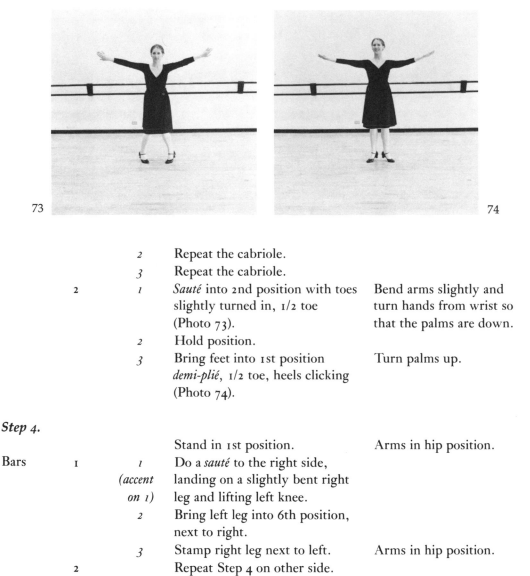

73   74

		2	Repeat the cabriole.	
		3	Repeat the cabriole.	
	2	*1*	*Sauté* into 2nd position with toes slightly turned in, 1/2 toe (Photo 73).	Bend arms slightly and turn hands from wrist so that the palms are down.
		2	Hold position.	
		3	Bring feet into 1st position *demi-plié*, 1/2 toe, heels clicking (Photo 74).	Turn palms up.

Step 4.

			Stand in 1st position.	Arms in hip position.
Bars	I	*1* (accent on 1)	Do a *sauté* to the right side, landing on a slightly bent right leg and lifting left knee.	
		2	Bring left leg into 6th position, next to right.	
		3	Stamp right leg next to left.	Arms in hip position.
	2		Repeat Step 4 on other side.	

Step 5.

			Stand in 3rd position, right leg in back.	Arms in hip position.
Bars	I	*1*	Brush right leg out *effacé en arrière;* beat left leg in cabriole *en arrière*.	

	2	Step on right leg in *en dehors* movement, continue circle,		
	3	stepping on left leg.		
2	1	Brush right leg out into	Keep left arm in hip position.	
	2	*arabesque, demi-plié croisé* (Photo 75).	Move right arm with open palm to *en avant* and *effacé.*	
	3	Do a *temps levé* on right leg in *demi-plié arabesque.* Repeat on other side.		

Step 6.

Stand in 3rd position, right foot in front.   Arms in hip position.

Bars	1	1	Step sideways on right leg.	
		2	Bring left leg in semicircle over right wth a small *sauté* (similar to *grand jeté en tournant*), turning 1/2 way to the right side to face backstage, with right foot in 4th position *en arrière*, toes on floor (Photo 76).	Cross arms over chest *en avant*, looking over right shoulder.
		3	Continue turning to the right to face forward again, left leg in *demi-plié*, right leg extended to *devant*, heel only on floor, toes pointing up (Photo 77).	Open arms to *à la seconde*, palms up. (Boys usually brush back of hand over the pointed toe.)
	2		Continue in same direction.	

Step 7.   Pas marché   3/4

Stand in 3rd position, right foot in front.   Arms in hip position.

Bars	1	1 (accent on 1)	Stamp strongly with right leg, *demi-plié*, and brush left leg slightly *effacé devant*.	Bring left arm over *devant* to *seconde*, palm open, left shoulder open.
		2	Step on left leg, 1/2 toe.	Bring outstretched arm slowly back into hip position with elbow well forward.

75

76

77

		3	Bring right foot to left with full foot on floor.	
2		1	Stamp with left leg, *demi-plié*, and brush right leg to *effacé devant*.	
		2,3	Continue Step 7 to the right.	

Step 8.

			Stand in 6th position.	Arms in hip position.
Bars	1	1	Stamp slightly to right on right leg and lift left leg, with bent knee, off the floor.	Turn head to right.

		2	Kick floor with left heel, lifting left knee high.	
		3	Hop on right leg once while left leg is lifted.	
	2		Repeat Step 8 on other leg with head turned to left.	

Step 9.

Stand in 3rd position, right foot in front.

Arms in hip position.

Bars	I	*1*	Step with right leg *devant*, *temps levé*, and bring left leg to *sur le cou-de-pied devant*.	Open arms over *en avant* to *à la seconde*, palms open.
		2	Do a *chassé devant* with left leg.	
		3	Do a *temps levé* in *arabesque demi-plié* (Photo 78).	Close arms back into hip position (still open in Photo 78).
	2		Repeat Step 9, starting again with right leg.	

To alternate sides, after the *arabesque:*

	3	*1*	Do another *temps levé* on the left leg, while bringing right foot *sur le cou-de-pied devant*.
		2	Do a *chassé devant* with right leg.
		3	Do a *temps levé* in *arabesque demi-plié*.

THE DANCES

Part Two

3. The Polka

Foremost among the great variety of Czechoslovakian dances is the Polka, a lively dance in 2/4, with the accent on the first beat, or the Polka Mazur, in 3/4, with the accent on the third beat. The Polka (for "Polish girl" or "Polish dance") is a chain or half-step dance, which originated in Bohemia about 1825 and became very popular in the ballroom of western European society. The Polka has influenced many other dances, and some form of it is danced throughout Europe today. It is the most popular dance in Czechoslovakia apart from the many dances performed on ceremonial occasions such as religious holidays, weddings, and harvest celebrations.

The Polka described here is from the opera *The Bartered Bride* by Bedrich Smetana (1824–1884). The opera was first performed in Prague on May 30, 1866. The Polka occurs at the end of the first act. The scene is a Bohemian village.

POLKA

From *The Bartered Bride*
Music by B. Smetana
2/4

Choreography by J. Pagels
For six to eight couples and a
solo couple.

Introduction, Bars 1–25: The *corps de ballet* couples run onto the stage, one after the other, greet one another, and then go into the dance formation: three couples in the front row downstage and three more couples in a second line behind them. The boys stand to the left of the girls.

Step 1.

Bars			
26–33	Couples in front line move toward stage location 8, couples behind toward location 6:	Hands behind back.

Starting with right (left) foot, bring right heel to *effacé devant* and lower onto full foot while the left foot closes to right.	Bring right shoulder slightly forward.
Repeat starting with other leg.	Bring left shoulder slightly forward.

Repeat Step 1 five times, alternating sides.

Stamp right, left, right.	Bring hands into hip position.

Step 1a.

34–41   Reverse movement of Step 1, starting with the other leg and moving to opposite side of stage.

The Polka

Step 2.

42–45	Partners turn to face each other and do the following step upstage toward 7: Step to the side with right (left) foot, heel touching the floor first, while doing a little hop on the left. Close left foot to right in demi-1/2 toe behind with a little hop on right. Immediately release right foot from the floor (a polka *chassé* or skip).	Hands on hips, heads turned slightly upstage but still looking at partner.
	Repeat Step 2 with the same leg five times.	
	Stamp right and left.	Open arms over *en avant* to *seconde*, palms open.

Step 3.

46–49	Moving in a circle, partners hop-skip seven times to the right around each other, starting with the inside leg. Stamp left and right.	Partners hook right elbows and stretch outside arm *en haut*. Open arms *à la seconde*, palms open.

Step 3a.

50–53	Repeat Step 2 downstage.

Step 4.

54–57	Do seven alternating polka steps, as in Step 1, forming three squares. Stamp right and left.	Arms behind the back.

Step 5.

58	With right leg, take one large step to the right and close the left foot to right, maintaining design of the squares.	Hands in hip position. Face inside of square.
59–61	Repeat sideways stepping three times.	

Step 5a.

62	With right leg, take one large step on the diagonal, away from the square, and close left foot to right.	Open arms *à la seconde*, fully stretched, palms open.
63	Repeat Step 5a, doing a 1/2 turn and starting with left leg, closing right to left and continuing to move on the diagonal, enlarging the squares.	

Step 5b.

64–65	Reverse Step 5a, back to the original dimensions of the squares.

Step 5c.

66–67	Step with right leg toward center of the square, and close left to right. Repeat, starting again with right leg and closing left.	Face inside of the square, hands behind the back.

Step 5d.

68–69	Repeat Step 5c, moving slightly forward.	Dancers' heads almost touch.

Step 5e.

70–72	Stand still.	With large movement, bring arms from behind the back over *seconde* to *en haut*. Bend forward toward one another in an embracing movement.

Step 6.

73–89	Couples move out of the squares, form a double line, and move in a half-circle through 1, 4, 7, and stage center to location 5, doing one polka step (Step 1) to the right and one to the left.	Hands behind the back.

Make an immediate 1/2 turn to face the audience and hop-skip backwards four times, alternating legs.

Bring arms *en avant*, stretched, and open them *à la seconde* with palms open.

Immediately turn in direction of circle and do two polka steps.

Arms behind the back.

Do four *chaînés* to the right, doing a *demi-plié* and a quick hop on right leg while lifting the left knee; body makes a 1/2 turn. Repeat the *chaîné* for another 1/2 turn. Repeat *chaînés* right and left.

Arms in hip position or opening and closing slightly in front of the body during the turns.

Repeat all of Step 6.

Step 7.

90–97 First three couples do the following step after a quick 1/2 turn toward 7; other couples continue as before toward 5:

Arms in hip position.

Do eight character *pas de basques* with slightly lifted, turned-in knees, moving slightly from side to side.

Arms can be opened over *en haut* to *à la seconde* on the first *pas de basque* and close again to hip position on the second *pas de basque*.

First three couples pass inside, the others outside; or the couples may criss-cross.

Dancers give each other their hands as they cross.

Step 8.

98–99 First couple moves to the right, boy in front, leading the girl. Second couple moves to the left in the same manner. The two lines move through corners 3 (or 4) to downstage, where they pass each other and form two lines, as in the Introduction:

	Place right heel *effacé devant* with a slight hop.	Left hand in hip position.
	With another small hop bring right foot back and in front of the left foot, toes only touching the floor.	Open right arm *devant* along with the foot movement, palm open. Bring right hand to left hand on left hip.
	Do two polka *chassés:* Bring right foot *effacé devant* on the floor with a slight hop; with another hop close left foot in 1/2 toe position behind right; open right *effacé devant* with full foot on the floor.	
	Repeat Step 8 on the left side.	Reverse arm movement.
100–117	Repeat Step 8 eight times, alternating sides.	

Step 9.

118–121	In a quick movement, hop on left leg while placing right foot *croisé devant*, toes pointed. With another quick hop on the left, move the right foot to *effacé devant*, toes pointed. With another quick hop on the left leg the right foot closes next to the left.	Arms in hip position.
	Repeat Step 9 with left leg.	
	With one *pas de basque*, partners turn to face each other; with another *pas de basque* they face the audience again.	Arms open over *en haut à la seconde* and then close into hip position again.

Step 9a.

122–125	Jump into 6th position *devant* onto the heels, step back onto 1/2 toe with right foot, then follow with left foot.	Arms stretched *en avant*, palms up, and hands bent up. Draw right arm to body, paralleling leg movement, palm still open

70

		and hand bent up. Repeat with other arm paralleling movement of left leg.
	Repeat Step 9a twice. Stamp right, left, right in small 1st position and immediately *pirouette en dedans* on left leg, with right knee turned in.	Arms in hip position. Then left arm *en dedans*, right *à la seconde*, and both close *en avant*.
118–125 (repeat)	Repeat Steps 9 and 9a.	

Step 10.

| 126–136 | Boy lifts girl up and sets her down on his left side, slightly in front of him, holding her at her hips. Boy does one *temps levé* looking over girl's right shoulder and another looking over her left shoulder, while girl looks in the opposite direction. Repeat the lift and the two *temps levé* to the other side; this time girl turns her head to look into boy's face. All link arms, and with four small hops make a circle. | |

Step 11.

| 137–144 | Couples split up, one group, in single file, goes left, the other right, to stage location 7: Doing 12 *chaînés*, hopped in polka style, form an alley from 2 to 3 and from 1 to 4, paralleling sides of stage. | Hands in hip position. Wave arms at solo couple, now arriving. |

Step 12.

| 145–152 | Solo couple enters from location 3 or 7, takes position at 7, and | Solo couple holds hands. |

71

moves from 7 to 5 with girl on
right, boy on left:

Starting with inside leg forward do one polka step.	Bring inside shoulder forward.
Do one polka step with outside leg, half turning away from each other.	Bring outside shoulder forward, still holding partner's hand, while other hand swings freely *à la seconde*.

Repeat the polka step right and
left.

Solo boy and girl each do a *failli, coupé,* and *grand pas de chat en tournant* separately.	Drop hands and bring arms over *en haut* to *à la seconde*.

Repeat to other side.

153–156   Facing 5, *sauté* on left leg, bringing right leg to *effacé devant*, heel only touching the floor, toes well lifted. Do another *sauté* while bringing right foot into a loose *sur le cou-de-pied* position, toes only touching the floor, in front of left foot. Do two polka steps *effacé devant*.   Hold hands criss-cross in front.

Repeat *sautés* with other leg.

Step 12a.

157–162   Solo couple does polka *chaînés* to center in preparation for the group, which forms a circle around them.

Solo boy lifts solo girl onto his shoulder.

Step 13.

163–178   Solo couple: Boy lifts girl onto his right shoulder. He turns to the right for 8 bars, to his left for 7 bars, then lets her down to the floor.

72

The group: Boys hold wrists and lock hands; girls sit on their hands, facing outside of circle. Boys walk in circle to the right for 4 bars, stop, then swing girls front and back for 4 bars.	Girls hold onto boys' shoulders.

Repeat to the other side, then girls slide off their perches.

Step 14.

179–182   Break the circle and form two small circles right and left. Solo couple moves to location 5.

Step 15.

183–190 Each boy turns his partner around, boy doing a *tombé* with right foot and *coupé* with left foot behind. Reverse the movement. Solo couple does same turn by itself.	Boy's left arm around girl's waist; girl's right arm around boy's waist. Free arms stretched *en haut*.

Step 16.

191–194 Couples form two lines as indicated in diagram, facing front, with solo couple in the center in front of them, all doing the following: Step on right foot *devant*, doing a small *sauté* and sliding back slightly while lifting left leg, then with left leg turned in, do a *demi passé* forward, passing the right leg. Place left leg *devant* and repeat, passing with the right leg *devant*. Repeat Step 16 three times.	Bring arms *devant*, stretched and with palms open. Then move *à la seconde* and place hands on hips. (One movement during the 4 bars of leg work.)

Step 17.

195–198 All dancers do a slight *sauté* on left leg, while right heel is placed *devant*, toes well lifted.	Hands in hip position; look to left.

Do another small *sauté* while right leg, turned in, passes the left leg and the right toes touch floor behind.	Look to right.
Hop again on left foot, then stamp floor right, left, right.	Look forward.

Repeat step with other leg, then repeat both sides again.

Step 18.

199–206

Each dancer separately:	
Brush right leg, turned in, to *à la seconde*, doing a *demi-plié* on left leg.	Stretch both arms to *à la seconde* on the right side, fingers stretched. The head follows the movement.
Bring right leg back and next to left in 6th position, both legs rising onto 1/2 toe. Lift left foot briefly and place it back on floor in 1/2 toe. Lift right foot off the floor briefly in 1/2 toe, and then slide left leg *à la seconde*, while right is doing a *demi-plié* (as in *pas de bourrée*).	Lower arms to *en bas*.
Repeat Step 18 to left.	Reverse arm and head movements.

Repeat Step 18 six times, alternating left and right.

Step 19.

207–214

Boy soloist does a *tombé* on right foot and *coupé* on left foot behind, thus turning his partner, who lifts her legs off the floor and stretches while being turned.	Girl soloist holds her partner's neck while boy holds her upper arms (or waist) in support.
Other dancers separately: Turn on the spot to the left with *tombé*, *coupé*, eight times.	Left arm across chest in front, right stretched *à la seconde*.

Step 20.

215–219   Front line does a polka *chassé*, leaving stage right. Back line leaves stage left in the same manner. Soloists jump off to right at location 1 on the last beats of the music.   Arms *à la seconde*.

THE POLKA

Intro.	1)	1a)
X X X X X X X X X X X X	→ → → ← ← ←	← ← ← → → →
2)	3)	3a)
X X X X X X X X X X X X ↓ ↓ ↓ ↓ ↓ ↓	↺ ↺ ↺ ↺ ↺ ↺	↑↑ ↑↑ ↑↑
4)	5)	5a.b.c.d.e.)

X X X X
  X X X X
    X   X
    X X		

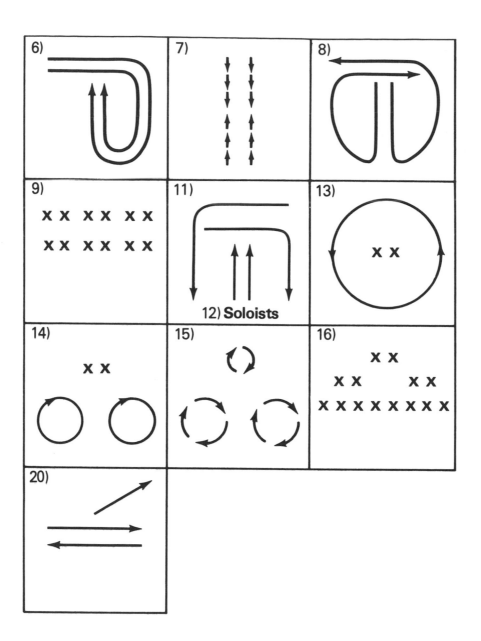

POLKA FROM *THE BARTERED BRIDE*

MUSIC BY FREDERICK SMETANA, Libretto by Karl Sabina,
English Translation by Rosa Newmarch

CHARACTER DANCE

CHARACTER DANCE

CHARACTER DANCE

Bas-ses rum-bling, cym-bals chink-ing, Rings of dan-cers in-ter-link-ing,

earth spins round us like a mill, and............................ our feet will

not keep still!............................

4. The Trepak

Russian dances show a vast variety of steps and movements, each quite distinctive and original. They are usually named for the villages in which they are danced. The oldest dance reported is the Chorowod, a group dance in circles and lines. There are special dances for the men, to show off their strength, athletic talents, and technique with intricate steps and high leaps; while the women mostly stay earthbound, in lovely soft and flowing movements or small, quick, temperamental steps. Humor, fun, and mime play major roles in all the dances, which are strong in expression and emotion. There are hundreds of Russian dances, for dance is part of every Russian's life—a daily diet—and occasions to dance are numerous. There is no doubt that the Russians are the most gifted character dancers of all.

The Trepak, a Russian dance in 2/4, is from the ballet *The Nutcracker*, with music by Peter Tchaikovsky and story by the famous E. T. A. Hoffmann. It was originally choreographed by Lev Ivanov. The first production was given by the Russian Imperial Ballet on December 17, 1892 in St. Petersburg. The ballet belongs to the classical repertoire of every company and has gained worldwide popularity. The Trepak belongs to the second act and the "Kingdom of Sweets." Today, there are a great many choreographies of the Trepak. The choreography described here is for an exceptionally skilled male soloist.

TREPAK

From *The Nutcracker*
Music by P. Tchaikovsky
2/4

Choreography by J. Pagels
For male solo

Preparation: Stand in 6th position in corner 2, facing stage position 1. Arms in hip position.

CHARACTER DANCE

Step 1.

Bar	I	*1*	Step onto right leg *effacé* in *demi-plié* with a strong stamp, brushing left leg *croisé devant demi-en l'air*.	Open arms wide to *à la seconde*, palms open.
		and	Step on left leg to 4th position *devant*.	Fold arms on chest.
		2	Step on right leg to 4th position *devant* (running steps).	
		and	Bring left leg forward to 4th position.	Open arms wide to *seconde*, palms open.

Step 2.

| | 2 | | Repeat Step 1, starting with left leg, then right leg, then left leg again, while continuing to move toward location 1, then move in a semicircle upstage to center stage. | |
| | 3–4 | | Repeat Step 1 twice, alternating sides. | |

Step 3.

| | 5–7 | | Starting with right leg, take 6 running steps with heels kicked up high behind the body. | Arms folded over chest. |
| | 8 | | Stamp right, left, right. | |

Step 4.

| | 9–12 | | Repeat Steps 1 and 2 twice. | |

Step 5.

| | 13–16 | | Repeat Step 3. | |

Step 6. **Prissjadka**

	17		Go into a deep knee bend in 6th position.	Arms folded over chest.
	18		Rise, opening to 2nd position, landing on heels only.	Open arms *à la seconde*.
	19–20		Repeat Step 6.	

THE AUTHOR DANCING THE TREPAK

Step 7.

21	*1*	Do a *grand plié* in 6th position.	
	2	Remaining in 6th position, lift right leg with bent knee *croisé devant* of left.	Slap right heel with left hand, while right arm is *en haut en arrière*.
22	*1*	Place right leg back in *plié in* 6th position.	
	2	Lift left leg *croisé devant* of right.	Slap left heel with right hand, while left arm is *en haut en arrière*.
23–24		Repeat Step 7.	

Step 8.

25–26	Do one prissjadka into small 2nd position.	Open arms *à la seconde*.
27–28	With next one do a *pirouette en dedans* on right leg with turned-in knee.	Fold arms *en avant*.
29–32	Repeat Step 8 to left. Add one prissjadka, then stamp right, left, right.	

Step 9. **Waddle**

33–44	Circling through 1, 8, 4, 7, 3, 6 to stage center, in a deep knee bend: Go into 6th position *grand plié*. With bent knee, bring left leg over *à la seconde* in *rond de jambe à terre en dedans en face* of right. Repeat with right leg. Repeat, alternating legs.	Arms crossed over chest.

Step 10.

43–48		Stand up and walk with four steps to center stage:	
	1	Place right heel *devant*.	Bring left arm across chest, right arm *à la seconde*.
	and	Then full foot.	

88

THE WADDLE

2   Lift left leg, with bent knee, *en arrière*, and do a *demi-plié* on right leg.
Repeat with left foot.
Repeat with right foot.
Stamp hard with left, right, left in 6th position *demi-plié*.

Reverse arms.
Reverse arms.
Open arms to *en avant* over *en bas*, parallel to each other, with palms open in bidding gesture.

THE RASTIAZKA

Step 11. **Rastiazka**

49	*1*	Go into 6th position *grand plié*.	Fold arms across chest.
	2	Jump high from 6th position, opening the legs into *effacé/à la seconde* with stretched knees and feet.	Bend as far forward as possible, opening arms parallel to legs and touching feet with fingertips.
50	*1*	Land in *grand plié* in 6th position and rise slightly, hopping a little on 1/2 toe.	Cross arms over chest.
	2	Go back into deepest *plié*.	
51–52		Repeat Step 11.	

Step 12.

53	Turn body toward location 8 and jump up, lifting both legs, knees bent *en arrière*, toes pointed.	Throw arms *en haut* and *en arrière*, arch body back (as in a *soubresaut*).
54	Land and rise.	
55–56	Take 4 running steps to corner 1.	

Step 13. **Cartwheel**

57	*1*	Go into *grand plié* in 6th position with knees closed, body bent forward and to the right.	Place the right hand on the floor to support the body.
	and	Continue turning to the right in *grand plié*, 1/2 toe over *en dehors*, body arched back strongly.	Support the body with right hand on the floor.
	2	Complete cartwheel on the floor.	Support the body with left hand on the floor.
58–64		Repeat Step 13 seven times, in a semicircle, and finish in corner 2.	

Step 14.

65	*1*	Facing location 8, go into *grand plié* in 6th position.	Arms *à la seconde*, palms open. Then fold across chest.
	2	Rise into *demi-plié* on right leg, with left leg kicked forward as in *frappé* and stretched *en avant*.	
66	*1*	Go back into 6th position *grand plié*, heels off the floor.	
	2	Rise into *demi-plié*, on left leg, *frappé en avant* with right.	
67–68		Repeat Step 14.	

Step 15.

		Stay in 6th position *grand plié* facing location 5. Do a Cobbler Step *en avant demi en l'air:*	Body leans forward.
69	*1*	Without rising, stretch right leg *en avant*, while left leg is in *grand plié*, 1/2 toe.	
	and	Bring right leg back into 6th position.	
	2	Stretch left leg *en avant*.	Open arms slowly to *à la seconde*.
70–72		Repeat Step 15 three times, alternating legs.	

Step 16. **Coffeegrinder**

73–82   Fall forward in 6th position, *grand plié*, 1/2 toe.   Support body with both arms.

Stretch left leg *en arrière-arabesque* on floor.

Bring left leg in *rond de jambe en dedans à terre* to *seconde* and *en avant*.

Pass left leg *en avant* in *rond de jambe*.   Lift left hand, then place it back on floor; lift right hand and place back.

Continue *rond de jambe* over *croisé devant*, lifting right leg, keeping knee bent, and letting left leg pass to complete circle.   Bring body well forward and support with both arms.

Repeat Step 16 nine times.

Step 17.

83   Rise, facing front in 6th position, feet slightly apart.   Arms *en bas*.

Step 18.

84   Stamp right, left, right coming slightly forward.   Raise arms parallel to *en avant* with palms open, open arms slightly.

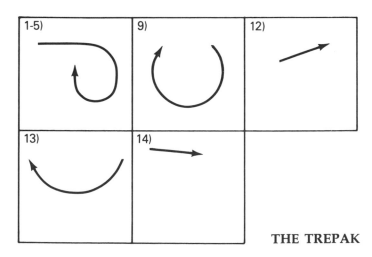

THE TREPAK

TREPAK FROM *THE NUTCRACKER*

PETER TCHAIKOVSKY

The Trepak

95

5. The Kazanski Tatari

The second Russian dance is a Kazanski Tatari, a peasant dance of the Tartar region. It is a comic dance for two girls and two boys. The boys in their Sunday finery come upon two girls and try to impress them with their dance skills. The girls pretend to be impressed and disappear suddenly while the two boys are outdoing each other in leaps and fancy steps.

KAZANSKI TATARI

Music traditional   Choreography after O. Harmoš
2/4   For two couples

The girls start in corner 4 at the beginning of the music. The boys start in corner 3 and circle over stage location 7 to 5 on the repeat of the music.

Step 1.

Bars			
	1	Girls do a *pas de basque* with lifted knees on right leg.	Hook arms and lean back.
	2	Repeat with left leg.	
	3–4	Take four running steps with body bent forward and heels kicked up *en arrière*, small and light.	Turn heads toward one another as if talking together.

Step 2.

	5–16	Repeat Step 1 three times and on last bar stamp right, left, right.	Open arms *demi à la seconde*.

| 1–16 (repeated) | Boys do the same steps but with knees lifted higher and the four running steps much heavier. Repeat Step 1 three times and stamp right, left, right on last bar, ending up next to a girl. While waiting for the boys, girls stand in 1st position, *demi-plié*, with toes open. | Hook arms, hands holding edge of vest.

Open arms in *demi à la seconde*. |

Step 3. Gormoshka (Harmonica) (2nd repeat of music)

Bars	1	Turn on left heel, bringing toes inward; at the same time turn on right toes to bring right heel out. Then turn on right heel and bring left toes back to original position. (This step resembles the American "Big Apple.")	Hands in hip position.
	2	Repeat.	
	3–4	Repeat twice. Girls look over their outside shoulders at the approaching boys; one girl moves to the right side, the other to the left.	

Step 4.

| | 5–8 | Repeat Step 3 coming toward each other. | Hands in hip position. |

Step 5.

| | 9–16 | Repeat Step 3 twice, moving away from each other—no longer looking at each other. | |

Step 6. (3rd repeat of music)

| | | Boys and girls together, one couple moving toward location 1, the other toward 3 (or toward 8 and 6). | All hook elbows, with the girls in the middle between the boys. |
| Bars | 1 | Do a waltz step with lifted knees. | |

	2		With next waltz step girls do a 1/2 turn in front of boys, ending up on the outside.	Unhook arms. Hook arms again.
	3		Waltz step toward 3 (1).	
	4		Waltz step with 1/2 turn for the boy.	
	5–16		Repeat Step 6 three times.	

Step 7. **(4th repeat of music)**

			Boys, starting from 6th position:	Hands in hip position.
Bars	1	*1*	Go into a *grand plié* with the knees only halfway open, feet together, 1/2 toe.	
		2	Lift right leg in *grand plié croisé devant.*	Slap right sole with left hand, right arm *en haut.*
	2	*1*	Hop in *grand plié* back into 6th position.	Open arms *à la seconde.*
		2	Lift left leg (from knee) in *grand plié croisé devant.*	Slap left sole with right hand, left arm *en haut.*
	3–6		Repeat Bars 1–2 twice.	
	7–8		Stand up; do one *pirouette en dedans* turned in, with right (left) leg lifted.	Fold arms across chest.
			Stamp left, right, left.	Open arms *à la seconde.*
			At the same time as boys:	Arms in hip position.
Bars	1	*1*	Girls do *pas de bourrée:* open right leg to *demi à la seconde* while going into *demi-plié* on left.	Girls look at boys in front of them.
		and	Bring right leg back to left in 6th position, releasing left leg from the floor.	
		2	Place left leg next to right.	
	2		Repeat on other side.	
	3–7		Repeat 5 times, alternating sides.	
	8		Stamp right, left, right.	Open both arms to *à la seconde.*

9–11	Boys and girls, passing each other on the diagonal:	
	Bring right (left) leg out to *à la seconde*, heel only touching the floor, toes well lifted, while left (right) leg is bent in *demi-plié*. Shift weight slightly to right (left) heel and bring left (right) leg in *demi-plié* to 3rd position next to right (left) leg. Repeat five times.	Boys hold left hand behind the neck, right hand in hip position. Girls keep hands in hip position.
12	Turn on right (left) heel and do a *pirouette en dedans*.	All bring arms *demi en avant*.
13–15	Repeat Bars 9–11 to the other side.	
16	Stamp right, left, right (left, right, left) in 6th position.	Arms open *demi à la seconde* and slightly *en avant*, palms open.

99

Step 8.   *(5th repeat of music)*

			Boys, turning in opposite directions:	Hands behind lower back.
Bars	I	*1*	Do a *sauté* on right (left) leg and land in *demi-plié*.	
		2	Stamp with left leg (right) in 2nd position, doing a quarter turn.	
	2–12		Continuing in same direction, repeat Step 8 eleven times.	
	13–16		Take four running steps and *temps levé* to partner at location 7.	

			At the same time, girls stand in 6th position, then:	Hands in hip position.
	I	*1*	Jump into 2nd position.	
		2	With another *sauté* bring right leg behind in *coupé*.	
	2–12		Repeat eleven times.	
	13–16		Run to the boys at location 7.	

Step 9.   *(6th repeat of music)*

		One couple moves over locations 5, 2, 6, to center stage; the other over 5, 8, 7, to centerstage.
Bars	1–16	Do Step 1 twice. Repeat again but do only one *pas de basque* and 12 running steps.

Step 10.   *(7th repeat of music)*

			Boys and girls move in one line sideways from 6 to 8 and from 8 to 6.	
			Boys stand in 6th position.	Turn body to location 2, looking left, left arm *en avant* across chest, right arm *á la seconde*, making a fist.
		and	Do a small *temps levé* on left leg while right leg is lifted with the foot next to left knee, the right knee turned *croisé devant*.	
Bars	I	*1*	Bring right leg down alongside left as if bringing the leg back to 6th position, but before	Turn body to 1, change arms to other side, look right.

100

			reaching the floor, open the right leg to 2nd position, placing only the heel on the floor, with the leg turned out.	
		and	Step on left leg next to right.	Turn body toward 2; move arms accordingly.
		2	Lift right leg off the floor.	
		and	Continue with a small *temps levé* (*sauté*), bringing the right leg, as before, to *á la seconde*, etc.	
	2–7		Repeat Step 10 six times sideways.	
	8		Stamp 3 times in place.	
	9–16		Repeat entire sequence in opposite direction.	
Bars	1–7		At the same time girls do Gormoshka, as in Step 3 seven times.	
	8		Stamp 3 times.	
	9–16		Repeat in opposite direction.	

Step 11. *(8th repeat of music)*

	1–8		Boys repeat first half of Step 7 twice in circle outside (8 bends).	
	1–8		At same time girls repeat first half of Step 7.	

Step 12.

			Boys stand in 6th position:	Arms folded across chest.
	9		*Temps levé* twice on left leg while right leg is pulled up from the knee.	Bring left arm *en haut* while right hand slaps right knee twice.
	10		Repeat with other leg.	Reverse arms.
	11	*1*	Alternate by lifting right knee with *temps levé* on left leg.	Left arm *en haut*, slap with right hand.
		2	Lift left knee with *temps levé* on right.	Right arm *en haut*, slap with left hand.
	12	*1*	Lift right knee with *temp levé* on left.	Left arm *en haut*, slap right.
		2	Lift left knee with *temps levé* on right.	Right arm *en haut*, slap left.

101

13		Lift right knee with *temps levé* twice on left leg.	Left arm *en haut*, slap right knee twice.
14		Lift left knee, *temps levé* twice on right leg.	Right arm *en haut*, slap knee with left hand twice.
15	*1*	Lift right knee, *temps levé* once on left leg.	Left arm *en haut*, slap right knee with right hand once.
	2	Lift left knee, *temps levé* once on right leg.	Right arm *en haut*, slap left knee with left hand once.
16		Stamp left, right, left.	Arms open with palms open to *demi-devant*.
9–16		At the same time, girls do Gormoshka as in Step 3, four times to right side, three times to left, and stamp three times to finish.	Arms behind lower back.

Step 13. **(9th repeat of music)**

Bars 1–16   Repeat Step 6 (Waltz step), with right couple going to location 2, the left couple to 1, twice front and twice back. Come back to original places and change direction: right couple going to 3, twice front and twice back; left couple to 1, twice front and twice back.

Step 14. **(10th repeat of music)**

Bars 1–16   Boys do 12 *pas de basques* moving in circle over 1 to upstage 7. Girls do the same, circling over 2 and meeting boys upstage at 7.

Boys and girls come together at 5 with three more *pas de basques* and three stamps.

Step 15. **(11th repeat of music)**

Bars	1–8	Girls do *pas de bourrée à la seconde*, as in Step 7.	Both arms swing over *en bas* to the right and then to the left.
		Boys go into deep *plié* and walk in knee bend, each circling his partner. Stand up on Bar 7 and stamp three times in Bar 8.	Arms *à la seconde*.
	9–16	Boys and girls repeat Step 12.	

Step 16. **(12th repeat of music)**

Bars	1	1	Boys do deep *plié* in 6th position, knees slightly open.	Arms folded across the chest.
		2	Rise and open to 2nd position on heels only.	Open arms to *à la seconde*, palms open.
	2	1	Deep *plié* again.	Arms folded across chest.
		2	*Pirouette en dedans* on right leg while rising.	Close arms *en avant*.
	3–16		Repeat Step 16 seven times and stamp three times at end.	
			At same time girls do *pas de basque* right and left twice.	Open arms, palms open. Then clasp hands behind neck.
			Then look at the boys, put heads together as in a conversation, point fingers at them, laughing. Then run off stage at location 8.	

Step 17. **(13th repeat of music)**

Bars 1–16 Boys alone repeat Step 7 four times. Go into deep *plié* and stand up with *pirouette en dedans* four times. Then looking for the girls and realizing they have left, they each do a multiple *en dedans* character *pirouette* and, in their confusion, run off in the wrong direction, at location 3.

103

THE KAZANSKI TATARI

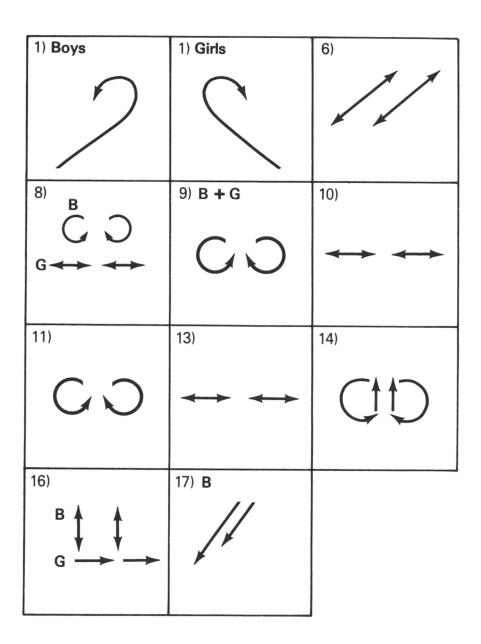

KAZANSKI TATARI

6. Csárdás

The Csárdás is a Hungarian dance, an Inn Dance in 4/4 and 2/4 timing with a slow *Lassu* or *Lassan* part and a fast *Friss* or *Gyors* part. Foreigners find it difficult to master both the steps and the character of the dance. There are heel clicks, stomps, fast turns, and kneebends. It is a very temperamental dance, with strong, forceful movements by the men followed by small, soft steps by the women, flirting with their partners. There is seldom a pattern to the dance.

The dance is naturally a peasant dance, *csárdás* meaning "innkeeper," and can be traced back to the Magyars of the ninth century. It also stems from the aristocratic Verbukos, one of the oldest dances of eastern Europe and the forerunner of the Csárdás. It became a national dance around 1840.

In the ballet *Coppélia*, the Csárdás follows shortly after the Mazurka in the first act. Franz is often seen dancing it with the villagers.

CSÁRDÁS

From *Coppélia*, Act I
Music by L. Delibes
4/4 for *Lassan*, 2/4 for *Friss*

Choreography by J. Pagels
For four or more couples and a
solo couple.

Solo boy enters from location 6 or 2, his partner from location 8 or 1. Other couples enter at the end of the introduction and join in the dance at Step 7.

Introduction. 4/4

| Bars | 1–2 | Solo boy: step on right leg *devant, temps levé* toward location 5. | Right arm *en avant*, left to *à la seconde*. |

106

	Repeat *chassé* with left leg, *failli* with right.	Reverse arms.
	Jump up, pulling up both knees.	Both arms *en haut*.
	Land in 6th position and stamp right, left, right.	Open arms *demi à la seconde*.
3–4	Solo girl: do same steps and meet boy at location 5.	
5-7	Boy walks over 2 to 7 and through center stage to 5; girl walks over 1 to 7 and 5. They wave at the appearing group, which places itself in a semicircle.	

79

Step 1.

	Soloists stand in 6th position.	Arms *à la seconde*, palms up.
8	Jump onto left knee facing 8, right leg *en avant* of left in 4th position (Photo 79).	Left arm *en avant*, right arm *en haut*.
	Get up immediately, place feet in 6th position.	Arms open *à la seconde*, palms up.

Step 2.

91	Step with right leg *croisé devant* of left facing location 2. Thrust left foot as in *frappé* to *effacé devant*, passing the right foot through 6th position parallel (Photo 80).	Left arm *en avant*, right arm high *à la seconde*, head facing 2.
	Bring left foot back, in same sharp movement, to front of right leg, the heel leading the movement (Photo 81).	
	Thrust left foot to *croisé devant* toward corner 1. While the body turns toward 1, bring the foot back to *effacé*, passing through 6th position with the heel leading.	Right arm *en avant*, left arm *à la seconde*, head facing 1.

80   81

	Turn left knee out, place left foot on right calf, and rise on right foot on 1/2 toe. Close both feet in 6th position, slightly open.	Arms *à la seconde*, palms down; head facing 5. Palms open.

Step 3.

10	Do a quick *chaîné* to the right onto left knee, turn quickly into reverse position onto right knee, facing 6. Stand up facing location 5 in 6th position. (Girl's *plié* not too deep.)	Left arm *en avant*, right arm *à la seconde*. Open arms *à la seconde*.

Step 3a.

11	Move right leg to *seconde*, knee turned in, heel lifted; left (supporting) leg is in *demi* 1/2 toe. Bring feet together, clicking heels. Bring left leg, with turned-in knee, to *seconde* and click heels with right leg. Repeat with right leg again.	Turn palms up and down with each heel click.

Step 4.

12–13		Repeat Steps 1 and 2 to left side.

Step 5.

	and	Hop on left leg, *frappé* to *effacé devant* with right.	Body leans well forward, head bent down, left arm *en avant*, right arm *à la seconde*.
14	*1*	Bring right leg *croisé devant*, toes only touching floor, across left leg (Photo 82).	
	and	With a little jump open both legs to *seconde*, turned-in, 1/2 toe.	Maintain body position; arms open to *seconde*, palms down.
	2	Snap heels together in 6th position, 1/2 toe.	Straighten body; turn arms so that palms are up.
	3–4	Repeat Step 5.	
15			

Step 6.

15		Repeat Step 3a four times in a circle to the left (right).

Step 7.

16–23		Repeat Steps 1–6, with other couples joining in.

Step 8. **Lassan**   4/4

		Stand in 6th position.	Arms *à la seconde*, palms open.
24	*1*	Stamp with right full foot to 2nd position (not turned out).	Arms remain *à la seconde*; head moves to right.
	and	Bring left foot to 6th position next to right.	
	2	Stamp with right again to *seconde*.	

110

82

and	Bring left foot next to right with a hard accent.	
3	Stamp with left foot to left *seconde*.	Arms remain open; head moves to left.
and	Bring right foot next to left in 6th position.	
4	Stamp with left foot to *seconde*.	
and	Stamp right foot with accent next to left in 6th position.	Arms remain open.

25	*1*	Stamp right in 6th position.	
	and	Stamp left in 6th position.	
	2	Stamp right in 6th position.	
	and	Stamp left in 6th position.	
	3	Stamp right in 6th position	
	and	Jump into *effacé* 6th position on full feet toward location 1.	Turn body toward 1; left arm *seconde*, right *en avant*.
	4	Jump into *effacé* 6th position on full feet toward 2.	Turn body toward 2; left arm *en avant*, right *seconde*.
	and	Jump into 6th position *effacé* toward 1 on full feet.	Turn body toward 1; left arm *seconde*, right *en avant*.
26–27		Repeat Step 8 starting on left side.	

Step 9.

and	Step on right full foot slightly *seconde*.	Right arm *en avant*, left arm *à la seconde*.

28	*1*	Kick left leg *croisé devant* with heel brushing the floor.	
	and	Step on left leg slightly *seconde*.	Left arm *en avant*, right arm *à la seconde*.
	2	Kick right leg *croisé devant* with heel brushing the floor.	
	3–4	Repeat Step 9.	

Step 9a.

| 29 | | Walk to the right in a small circle, taking 6 small steps, starting with the right foot, and end in 6th position. |

Step 9b.

| 30 | | Repeat Step 5 twice, starting with right leg. |

Step 10.

31	*1*	Step onto left leg with slightly bent knee. Bring right leg with bent and lifted knee *croisé devant* of left.	Always look in direction of working leg. Body inclines to left, left hand slaps right foot, while right arm is *à la seconde*.
	and	Right foot moves to *à la seconde*, the heel being the highest point, the knee turned in.	Slap right heel with right hand; left arm *à la seconde*.
	2	Bring right leg, with bent knee, *croisé derrière* of left leg.	Slap right foot with left hand; right arm *à la seconde*.
	and	Move right leg with bent knee, to *effacé en arrière*, the heel being the highest point.	Slap right heel with right hand; left arm *à la seconde*.

Step 11.

	3	Step back onto right leg.	Bring arms *en bas*.
	and	Close left to right.	
	4	Do a quick *grand plié* in 6th position.	
		Open into small 2nd position when rising.	Open arms *à la seconde*, palms open.

The music for Steps 7–11 should be played fast. The movements of Steps 10 and 11 are very fast!

Step 12.

32	*1*	Step on right leg *effacé devant*.	Left arm in hip position.
	2	Do a *développé* (very high) with left leg to *croisé* toward 1, while right leg does a *demi-plié*.	Bring right arm *en haut*.
	3	Step on left leg and go immediately onto the right knee, left leg in 4th position *en avant*, facing 1.	Bring right arm *en avant*, then *en bas*, and hold it up as in an *arabesque*.
	4	Stand up, bringing right leg to left, *demi-plié* (Photo 83).	Open left arm *à la seconde*; place right hand behind head.
33	*1*	Push off from left leg, bringing right leg to *à la seconde* in *demi-plié*; lift left foot and place it next to right (Photo 84).	Turn palm of left arm down and up again.
	2	Push off again on left leg, bringing right leg into *demi-plié à la seconde*.	Arms as before.
	3	Step with left foot *croisé* over right *devant*, bring the right heel up quickly to the side, with knee turned in.	Open arms to *à la seconde*, palms down.
	4	Clap heels together.	Turn palms up.
34–35		Repeat Step 12 to the left side, facing slightly toward location 2 (*écarté*).	

83

84

Step 13.

36–37	The partner on the left stamps with right leg into 4th position *en avant*, facing 8 (Photo 85).	Left arm *en haut*; right arm open *en avant*, palms up toward 8 and partner (offering hand).
	Partner on other side repeats movement.	Repeat arm movement in opposite direction, grasping hands.
	Girl turns into partner's arm with *chaîné*.	
	Girl unwinds from boy's arm; partners stand side by side.	

Step 14.

38–39	Repeat Step 5 three times, dancers turning in opposite directions to the outside.	
	Then take a big step back into 6th position, boy (girl) forward.	
	Boys move away from girls.	Hands behind back, relaxed.

Step 15. Friss 2/4 Girls only:

40–41	Stand with feet in 6th position, heels together, and move toward right side (Photo 86).	Arms move from *en bas* to *à la seconde*, to *en haut*, then behind the head.
42–45	Lift heels and bring them to the right.	Turn body slightly toward location 2.
	Place heels on floor.	
	Lift toes and bring them to the right.	Turn body slightly toward 1.
	Place toes on floor. (Knees stay together.)	Hands remain behind head.
	Repeat 3 times.	
46–49	Jump from left leg onto right with knees lifted high in *pas de basque*.	Arms open with palms up in *à la seconde*.
	Place left foot next to right in 6th position.	
	Lift right foot briefly and place it next to left.	

85

86

Repeat *pas de basque* to the left, then right, then left.

50–53	Repeat steps in Bars 42–45 to the left.	Place hands behind the head.
54-57	Repeat steps in Bars 46–49 to the left (4 *pas de basques* to left, right, left, and right), turning so that partners face each other facing location 8 (6).	Open arms *à la seconde.* Place hands in hip position.

The boys have been watching the girls and step toward them at their last *pas de basque.*

Step 16.

58	*1*	Stand in 6th position; do a *demi-plié* on left leg while brushing right leg out to *à la seconde demi en l'air* with turned-in leg (Photo 87).	Lower arms to *en bas;* swing both arms to right side.
	and	Bring right leg back to original position next to left leg; release left leg briefly (Photo 88).	
	2	Place left foot back in 6th position.	Bring arms *en bas.*
59–61		Repeat Step 16 to left, right, and left.	Swing arms to left side, right side, and left; then place them on partner's shoulders.

115

87   88

Step 17.

62	*1*	Boys jump with both feet held tight in 6th position toward 1, into 6th position.
	and	Hop back to original position.
	2	Jump in the same manner toward 4.
	and	Jump again in 6th position to original position.
63	*1*	Jump again in 6th position toward 1.
	and	Jump back to original position.
	2	Jump toward 4.
64–65		Repeat Step 17.

Step 18.

66–73   Boys repeat Steps 16 and 17. Girls do Steps 16 and 17 in opposite direction.

Step 19.

74–80   Bring right leg with turned-out knee onto 1/2 toe behind left leg, doing a little skip on left leg. Bring left leg behind right leg onto 1/2 toe with turned-out   Open arms in *à la seconde*, palms open. Gradually bring arms from *seconde* to *en avant*, turning palms down. Body leans forward.

116

89   90

knee, and skip lightly on right leg.

Repeat four times, moving backward toward location 7.

Repeat twice more, moving forward to location 5.   Bring arms back to *à la seconde*, opening palms.

Step 19a.

81–82   Do a small *temps levé* on left leg, lifting right leg over *demi-passé* to *croisé devant*. Stamp, release back leg, and stamp once. Do another small *temps levé* on left leg, bring right leg over *demi-passé*, bent up to *croisé derrière* behind left leg. Stamp with right *croisé devant* (Photos 89, 90).   Bring right arm to *en avant*, with left arm bent up behind body. Move left arm *croisé devant* in *en avant* position, while right arm goes over *à la seconde* to *en haut* behind head.

83–84   Repeat Step 19a.

Step 20.

85–88   Boys stand in 4th position, sideways to partners and flick their skirts.

Girls turn fast in place, to the right.   Arms in hip or *seconde* position, gradually lifted to *en haut*.

117

89–96   Repeat Steps 19a and 20.

Step 21. Cou-de-talon (not to be mistaken for a low cabriole)

97   Step with left *croisé* over right,   Cross arms *en bas*, look
             jump sideways toward location   over left shoulder with
             1 in *écarté*, gliding left foot over   head inclined. Open arms
             floor while right opens to   to *seconde* then bring them
             seconde, and bring left to right in   *en bas*.
             6th position.

98   Step again with left foot *croisé*   Repeat arm movement.
             devant over right, jump to side,
             opening right leg to *seconde*,
             sliding with left over floor again
             and closing in 6th position
             (Photos 91, 92).

99–100   Repeat.

Step 22. Holubetz

101–104   Step on right leg, do a small   Left (outside) arm *en haut*,
             temps levé on right leg, open left   right arm on hip or hooked
             leg slightly and beat heels in   in partner's elbow.
             cabriole. Do three more
             cabrioles, completing two
             circles to the right.

91   92

Step 23.

| 105–112 | Repeat Steps 21 and 22 toward location 2. | Partners separate after repeat. |

Step 24.

| 113–119 | Repeat Steps 19 and 19a, taking 8 steps to reach original place at center stage. Move back slightly with 7 of the same steps. | |

Step 25. Oborot

| 120–127 | Partners face each other. Turn together for 8 bars with small *temps levé* to the right, accent on count 1. | One arm around partner's waist, other *en haut*. |
| 128–133 | Stop, switch direction immediately, and do 6 *temps levé* to the left. | Switch arm positions. |

Step 26.

134	Boys stop. Girls do a *chaîné* to *seconde*.	
135	Girls go down on their right knee, sideways, and sit down, right leg bent, left leg stretched along on floor.	Left hand held by partner, right hand behind, supporting body on floor.
	Boy supports this fall by catching his partner's outstretched hand at the completion of her *chaîné* and letting her down gently.	
	Final pose: girl on floor, boy in 4th position with right leg *devant demi-plié*, left leg stretched *en arrière*.	Left arm *en arrière* and *en haut*.

CSÁRDÁS—FINAL POSE

Intro: Solo	6)	Group
8)	9a)	11-12)
15) **G's alone**	19)	21)
24)	25)	

CSÁRDÁS FROM *COPPÉLIA*

LÉO DELIBES

7. The Kolo

The Kolo is danced by many of the nationalities in Yugoslavia and other states. The rhythm can be 2/4, 3/4, 4/4, 5/4, 3/8, 4/8, 5/8, or 7/8, and is often strongly accented and syncopated.

In the Balkans, *Kolo* means a "wheel" or a "round" dance, a choral dance often performed as a chain. It is one of the few leaping dances among European folk dances. The Kolo appears in many countries, and, depending on the nationality, may be fast or slow. It is often accompanied by singers and instrumentalists, and presented as a dance for men or for couples. There are many different patterns and choreographic forms, but most often it is danced in circles and straight lines with the tempo changing frequently. There is much pantomime and solo dancing in the center.

The Yugoslavs love to dance and find many occasions to do so. The dance described here is a Tatovac, a wedding dance from Croatia, the northern part of Yugoslavia.

TATOVAC

Music traditional	Choreography after O. Harmoš
2/4	For one couple

Boy and girl start from center stage, holding hands. Girl is on the boy's right.

Introduction

Bars	1–4	Walk forward holding inside hands. Act shy with each other. Finish standing in 6th position.	Swing hands front and back, looking at each other and then away.

128

Step 1.

5–7 · Both step to right side with right foot, heel touching ground first in *effacé*.
Close left foot to right in *coupé* "under," *demi-plié.*
Step on right foot again and bring left foot in front of right with a *dégagé en l'air.*
Immediately pull left heel back to right ankle, *sur le cou-de-pied* (a *frappé* with accent toward supporting leg) (Photo 93).

Arm movements as in Introduction.

93

Step 1a.

8 · Step on left leg and repeat *frappé* movement *effacé devant* to the right. Step again on right leg and repeat to left.

Step 2.

9–12 · Repeat Steps 1 and 1a to left side.

Step 3. (repeat of music)

5–8 · Repeat Steps 1, 1a, and 2, but · Shake the entire body

129

94

double the number of steps to each side and *frappés* in the same number of bars.

during the *frappé* movement.

Step 4. (repeat of music)

9–12   Repeat Steps 1, 1a, and 2. Boy moves to the right and upstage, girl to the right and downstage in Step 1. Reverse directions in Step 2 (Photo 94).

Arms in reversed *port de bras* over 2nd position, *en haut* to the hips on first of each sideways step, hands making a fist.

Step 5. Eagle step

13   *1*   Step on right heel in partner's direction, *coupé* under with left foot.

Arms *en haut*, right arm higher than left.

2   Step on right foot again, and with left do a primitive *soutenu en dedans* (1/2 turn) in 1st position. Face partner again.

Bring arms over *en haut* to *en avant* and *en bas*, palms facing floor.

14   *1*   *Relevé* in 6th position and do two hops on *demi-pointe*.

Extend both arms to partner with finger tips almost touching.

2   Do a *demi-plié*.

15–16   Repeat two hops and *demi-plié*, moving to left so that partners'

Arms go back in reversed *port de bras* to the waist, fingers in front.

95

96

right shoulders face each other
(Photos 95, 96).

13–16	Repeat Step 5 (repeating music).	Finish with arms extended to partner and grasping hands, boy's fingers under girl's extended hands.
17–24	Repeat Step 5 twice more.	

Step 6.

25–40

Boy and girl face each other, and while doing a 1/4 turn, stamp hard on left foot, doing a *battement développé* to *effacé devant* with right leg (boy to location 7, girl to 5), bringing left shoulders together.

Left arm is fully stretched; right arm is at chest level with bent elbow.

Bring right leg to left leg; then step on left and do a 1/2 turn *(pas de bourrée).*

Right shoulders close together.

Do a *grand battement developpé* with left leg, right shoulders almost in contact.

Place right arm at shoulder height over partner's right arm. Extend left arm behind the head between *seconde* and *en haut*, stretched to the outside.

Repeat Step 6 to right and left again (4 *grand battement développé* and 3 *pas de bourrée* in all) (Photo 97).

Step on right leg *demi-plié*, *coupé* with left behind.

Look at each other and run in a circle, taking 8 right-left *coupé steps.*

Hold partner's right arm.

97

Make a 1/2 pivot turn to finish.
Boy finishes on right side of
stage, girl on left.

Repeat Step 6 with boy
finishing on left side of stage,
girl on right.

At end of last pivot boy's
hands go on girl's waist;
hers go on his shoulders.

Step 7.

41–42   Spring off both feet, lifting leg
in a turned-in *passé*. Land on
both feet in 6th position.
Girl is on *demi-pointe* and
demi-plié. Then boy helps her
jump to right and left with feet
together, making a 1/2 turn.

43–44   Repeat.

Step 8.

45–48   Repeat Step 7 to other side.

Step 9.

49–56   Repeat Steps 7 and 8 in more
vigorous manner and making
1-1/2 turns.

Step 10.

57–60   Boy does high *pas de basque* to
left and right, followed by 4
running steps (as in a *jeté*),
throwing the legs *derrière*. Work
in clockwise direction around
girl. Repeat, ending in opening
position on left side of girl.

Open arms to left and close
on hips at end of 2nd *pas de
basque*.

Boy stands as girl completes her own *petit pas de basques* on the
spot, replacing *jetés* with a pivot to the right, left, right, also
alternating direction of the *pas de basques*.

133

Girl turns to right in a *pas de bourrée* beginning with right foot.

Extend both arms to *en haut* and open, right arm higher. Boy catches hold of girl's left arm.

Girl returns with another *pas de bourrée* to finish in opening position.

Step *11*.

61–72   Repeat Steps 1, 1a, 2, and 3.

Step *12*.

73–76   Girl springs into 2nd position, then hops five times with left leg in *attitude devant* to the right. Meanwhile boy makes fun of her efforts.

Arms *en haut*.

73–76   Repeat Step 12 (repeat of music).

Step *13*.

77–80 (twice)   Boy continues to make fun of girl, as she repeats Step 12. Girl joins him in last part of sequence.

Step *14*.

81–82   Both work toward wings, boy counterclockwise, girl clockwise:
Boy steps on left foot and lifts right foot in *ballonné devant* with a small circle and toward the body.

Bring arms to *à la seconde*, lifted slightly higher, then place in hip position.

Do a turned-in *passé* and place foot in 6th position, hopping back slightly while bringing the feet together.
Take 3 running steps, right, left, right.

134

83–84	Repeat Step 14 three times, working to finish upstage and center.
81–84	Girl does same steps at the same time but starts with other leg.

Step 15.

85–88	Both step on right foot, holding hands.
	Repeat Steps 1 and 1a, left, right, left, right, *cou-de-pied devant*.

Step 16.

89–91	*Tombé* forward on outside foot (boy left, girl right), with other foot in 3rd position *à terre* on *demi-pointe*, pushing from behind.	Inside shoulders almost touching.
	Repeat Step 16 five times.	

Step 17.

92	Turn out and away from each other in *soutenu*.
	Boy falls on his knees, throws his arms around girl's waist; girl cradles his head.

Intro. +1)	2)	3)
4)	4)	5)
6)	10)	11)
14)	15)	16)

TATOVAC

137

8. The Tarantella

The Tarantella is an Italian dance, claimed simultaneously by Sicily (the Sicilian Tarantella), Naples (the Neapolitan Tarantella), and Sardinia. It is a dance of the low and middle classes; and, as is the case with all national character dances, it is used on such festive occasions as Easter, a wedding, or a harvest.

It is a very balletic dance in a rapid 6/8. Many of the classic ballet steps find their origin in the Tarantella. It is a gay, light, and springy dance with many hopping, spiderlike steps. The men snap their fingers, and the women beat and rattle their tambourines.

The name of the dance is explained in several ways. In one version, the name derives from the town of Taranto, in southern Italy, the home of the tarantula, a poisonous spider that moves in small hops. Another explanation attributes the name to the insect's bite. It was believed that vigorous dancing would drive out the poison.

The Tarantella described here is from the ballet *La Boutique Fantasque* ("The Fantastic Toyshop") to music of Rossini arranged by Respighi. In the ballet it is performed by a solo doll; here it is choreographed for couples.

TARANTELLA

Music by G. Rossini/O. Respighi   Choreography by J. Pagels
6/8   For two or four couples

Introduction.

Bars   1–4   Couples enter from stage locations 1 and 2 and move sideways on 1st beat of Bar 4. Girls hold tambourine on left hip with both hands (Photo 98).

98

Step 1.

		2*	Make a small jump with the right (left) leg *à la seconde*, 1/2 toe.	
Bar	5	*1*	Immediately bring left leg *croisé devant*, 1/2 toe, into small 4th position.	*Épaulement*, left shoulder forward, head turned to left.
		2	Make another small jump with right (left) leg *à la seconde*, 1/2 toe.	
	6	*1*	Bring left leg into *croisé derrière*, 1/2 toe.	Right shoulder forward, head turned to right.
	7–8		Repeat three times and hop on last count into 6th position.	
	8–12		Moving in opposite direction, make a small jump onto left leg in *à la seconde*, 1/2 toe.	
			Repeat Step 1 and on last count kneel on right (left) knee in location 2 (1), couples facing each other slightly.	Place tambourine on other hip; hold with right (left) hand.

Step 2.

13	*1*	Beat tambourine on floor (Photo 99).	Body leans forward.

---

*Most Tarantella steps start on the fouth eighth note of the measure.

		Beat tambourine on left (right)	
	2	knee (Photo 100).	
14	*1*	Beat tambourine on left (right) elbow (Photo 101).	
	2	Beat tambourine with left hand (Photo 102).	Body leans back slightly.
15–16			Open both arms over *en haut* and *à la seconde*, rattling tambourine.
17–18		Repeat first half of Step *2*.	
19–20		Get up from the floor, while rattling tambourine, and into 6th position.	

Step 3.

	Couples at location 2 move to the left, couples at 1 move right.	
21–23	Step onto left leg in *demi-plié*, right leg *attitude effacé en arrière*.	Tambourine in left hand, right *à la seconde*.
24	Hop in circles. Do a double *pirouette en dedans;* finish in 6th position. (Couples at location 1 in reverse.)	Close arms for *pirouettes* and change tambourine to other hand.
25–28	Repeat Step 3 to other side.	

Step 4.

		Move from location 2 to 1 (1 to 2) in straight lines:	Tambourine in left hand, right hand in hip position.
29	*1*	Step on right leg into *demi-plié arabesque*.	
	2	*Temps levé demi-plié* in *arabesque*.	
30–33		Repeat four times, doing 8 *temps levés*.	
34	*1*	Slide right (left) leg in *failli en avant*.	Bring right arm to *en avant*.
	2	*Contretemps*, left over right, changing direction back to location 2.	Change tambourine from right into left hand.
35–40		Repeat Step 4 to opposie side (Photo 103).	

103

104

105

106

Step 5.

		Moving in a large circle to the right (left), couples one behind the other:	Tambourine held at left side with both hands.
41	*1*	Step on right leg *demi-plié*, left leg *demi arabesque en arrière*.	
	2	Brush left leg in *battement en cloche* to *en avant* and do a small *temps levé* (Photo 104).	Bring both arms forward. Hold tambourine in left hand and clap it with right hand.
42	*1*	Step on left leg into *demi-plié en avant*.	Arms go into *à la seconde;* body leans forward.

146

	2	Brush right leg in *battement en cloche en arrière* and *temps levé* (Photo 105).	Slap tambourine behind body.
43–44		Take 4 running steps right, left, right, left; kicking heels up in back.	Body leans well forward. Tambourine held at left hip.
45–56		Repeat Step 5 three times to complete the circle. The last time take only 3 running steps, then step with right leg to *seconde*.	

Step 6.

	and	Swing left leg in *demi rond de jambe* over *seconde* to *en avant* (similar to a *grand jeté en tournant*), turning the body halfway around and leaning well forward (Photo 106).	Hold tambourine in right hand, both arms open to *seconde*.
57		End in 4th position, *demi-plié* on left leg, *allongé en arrière* with right.	Left arm *demi en haut*, right hand beats floor with tambourine, then right hand slaps left knee and left elbow.
58		Rise and bring legs together in 6th position.	
59–60		Raise and lower heel in 6th position.	Hold tambourine over head.
	and	Step with right leg into *demi seconde*.	Open arms *à la seconde*.
61–72		Repeat Step 6 to the right, left, and right. On last 2 bars couples face each other, boy facing 4, girl facing 2.	

Step 7.

| | | Boy's right leg in *attitude en arrière* to girl's leg in *attitude en avant*: | Hold waist with one arm, other *en haut* holding tambourine. |
| 73–76 | | *Sauté* toward location 2. Reverse positions. | |

77–80   *Sauté* backward to location 4
with 8 hops.

Step 8.

81–86   Couples separate, and with 12
running steps, form an open
circle. The girls run into the
center.

Step 9. Fouetté

		Girls in front, right foot in 3rd position *devant*.	
87		Bring right leg in *demi rond de jambe* over *à la seconde* with slightly bent right knee, placing right foot in 3rd position *en arrière*.	Right arm with tambourine swings along with right leg, over *seconde* to *en haut*, and is met by left hand, which slaps tambourine (Photo 107).
88	*1*	*Soutenu en tournant* on both legs to the right, *coupé en arrière* with left leg.	Open both arms to *à la seconde*.
	2	Step on left foot in 3rd position behind right.	Left arm *en bas*; right arm *en avant*.
89–94		Repeat *fouetté* three times.	
95–102		Girls and boys change places, with the girls, in back, moving back with simple *emboîté derrière* 8 times, and boys moving forward with *emboîté*. Repeat Step 9.	Hold tambourine *en haut*.

Step 10.

	Couples stand in a straight line facing opposite directions, left	Hook right elbows, hold left arm, with tambourine,

107

	(outside) leg in *attitude devant*, right (supporting) leg in *demi-plié:*	*en haut;* look at each other.
102–106	Hop 7 times in circle on supporting leg.	
	On 8th hop finish in 6th position.	Reverse arms.
106–109	Hop around each other in opposite direction.	
	Open up.	Unhook arms.
110	Stand in 6th position.	

Step 11.

111	*Ballonné* twice with right leg to *effacé devant*.	Both arms up, slap tambourine twice (Photo 108).
112	*Ballonné* twice on left leg.	Repeat.
113	Repeat with right leg and stay on left leg.	Repeat.
114	Jump to the side with right leg, 1/2 toe, in a *demi rond de jambe en l'air;* immediately bring left leg in *grand rond de jambe en l'air croisé devant* 1/2 toe in front of right, and do a *sotenu en tournant* to the right (Photos 109, 110).	Open arms into *à la seconde.* Arms *en haut.*
115–126	Repeat Step 11 to the left, to the right, and to the left again.	

Step 12.

126–134	Go down onto knee and repeat Step 2 twice. Get up.

Step 13.

	Moving from left to right (right to left):	
134–137	Do a small *temps levé* on left leg, bringing right to *seconde*, toes	Tambourine in left hip position (Photos 111, 112).

150

108   109

110   111

112   113

only touching the floor, toes
turned in.
Do a *temps levé* on left leg,
moving sideways; open right leg
in *seconde*, heel only touching the
floor, toes well lifted.
Repeat first *temps levé*.
Sauté into 6th position. Clap tambourine *en avant*.
Repeat Step 13 to other side.

138–139 Form one line in preparation for Step 14.

Step 14.

140–155 In circle over locations 2, 3, 4, Wave arms from side to
starting with right leg, side in front of body, *demi*
glissande-jeté 14 times, *en bas*, with the step (Photo
completing circle. Run for two 113).
counts to original position, as in
Step 1.

Step 15.

156–171 Repeat Steps 1 and 2.

Step 16.

172–175 Move toward location 5 in two Clap tambourine on last
lines: do 2 *chaînés* and *tombé*, beat.
pirouettes en dedans, and finish in
4th position.

THE TARANTELLA

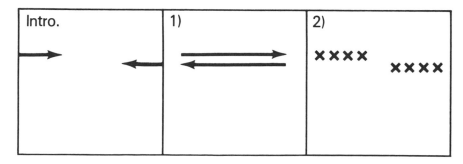

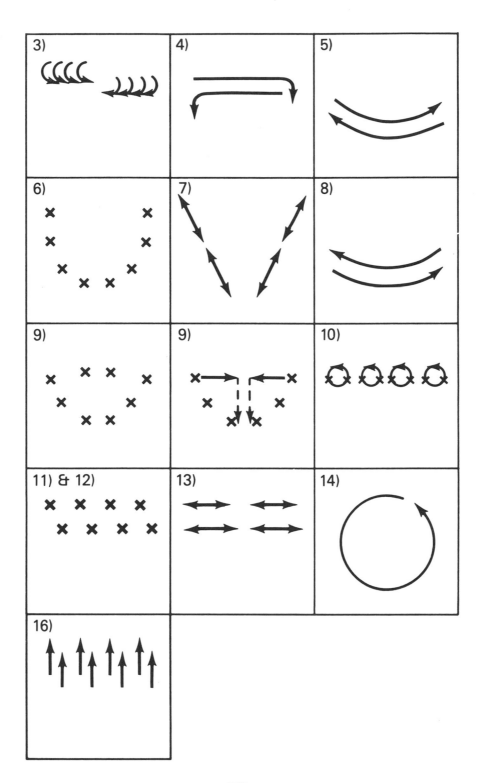

TARENTELLE FROM *LA BOUTIQUE FANTASQUE*

GIOACCHINO ROSSINI

Arranged by Ottorino Respighi

CHARACTER DANCE

CHARACTER DANCE

CHARACTER DANCE

9. The Mazurka

The Mazurka is a Polish national dance in 3/4 or 5/8 timing, with the accent usually on the second beat. It originated in the duchy of Mazovia and became very popular about 1850, although it dates back to the beginning of dance, specifically to the circle dance. It is danced in pairs. There are many Mazurka steps, perhaps more than in any other national dance. The steps are often quite difficult and include much stomping and heel clicking. The man's steps are forceful, the woman's much smoother. The arms are held high and stretched or the hands are placed on the hips with the elbows held forward.

There are a variety of Mazurkas in central and eastern Europe. Adopted by high society, the Mazurka became part of ballroom dance, where it showed elegance of style and movement. In the country it displayed a certain heaviness. Despite all, fluidity of movement remained.

Poland, in particular, has given the world quite a few dances that have infiltrated the ballroom. Apart from the Mazurka there are the Polonaise, the Polka-Mazur, and the Krakowiak, all of which are important to the professional theatre and its dance.

All these dances are group dances. There is no national costume; color and style vary from village to village. As in most eastern European countries, dance is a part of daily life and enjoyment. Any festive occasion will bring out the dancers.

The Mazurka described here comes from the ballet *Coppélia*, with music by Léo Delibes and book by Charles Nuitter. Saint Leon was the choreographer of the first presentation at the Paris Opera on May 25, 1870. Today, the ballet belongs to the classic repertoire of all major companies. The Mazurka is a highlight of the scene in the village square. It is usually performed by a group and Franz, with the Burgomaster joining them briefly.

CHARACTER DANCE

MAZURKA

From *Coppélia*   Choreography by J. Pagels
Music by L. Delibes   For six couples
3/4
The dancers enter from location 3. The dance starts with three couples in the front line and three couples behind them. All dancers have hands on hips. Bar 1, Introduction.

Step 1. *Mazurka step traveling forward*

Bars			
	2–9	Step forward on left leg and do a *ballonné* with the right leg, ending in *sur le cou-de-pied devant* of left leg. Brush the right leg out immediately in a *chassé devant*, the left forming an *arabesque*.	Girl places her forearm on her partner's forearm and holds his hand. Bring outside arm to *en avant* then *à la seconde*.
		Do one *temps levé* in *demi-plié* on the right leg.	Reverse arms.
		Continue with the other leg, starting with a *temps lié* on the right leg, while the left is brought *sur le cou-de-pied devant* of the right.	
	10–17	Repeat Mazurka step, starting with the right leg.	
		Follow with 4 *coupé pas de basques*, legs slightly bent at the knee, boy and girl facing each other and making one full circle to the right.	Outside arm *en haut*.
	2–17	Repeat Step 1 (to repeat of music), still moving forward and with the *pas de basque* circle always going slightly backward.	

Step 2. *Holubetz*

	18–21	Couples face each other and move diagonally in opposite directions:

162

Step with left leg *croisé devant* of right, brush right leg into *à la seconde*, *demi en l'air*, and beat left leg against right in *cabriole*. Repeat. Step again with left *croisé devant* of right and do two smaller *cabrioles*.

Sauté into 2nd position on 1/2 toe.

Arms in *à la seconde*, palms open and up.

Bend arms slightly in *seconde* and turn palms down, hands bent up at wrist.

Bring heels together in a sharp click.

Stretch arms again and turn palms back.

22–25   Repeat Step 2 to other side. At end of repeat boy does not click heels, but places left knee on floor.

Arms high *à la seconde*.

163

***Step* 2a.**

| 26–29 | Girl does 3 *pas de basque* behind the boy, starting with right leg. Then *sauté* into 2nd position and do one heel click. | Hands in hip position. |

| 30–33 | Boy stays on knee, girl repeats Step 2a from the left side, starting *pas de basques* with left leg, ending on the right side of the boy. | |

Step 3. **En tournant**

34-37	All couples move toward location 8:	
	Step on right leg into *demi-plié* and do a *demi rond de jambe en l'air* with left leg toward location 8, turning the body to face 6, and place left leg, partly stretched, behind the body, *pointe tendue.* Turn body over right shoulder to face the extended left leg. Left toes are pointed up and only the left heel rests on the floor.	Hands in hip position.
	Repeat on the same side, then do a *temps levé* on the left leg while turning the right leg in, so that the toes only are touching the floor and the body is turned slightly toward location 6. Do another *temps levé* on left leg; turn leg out again so that the heel only is on the floor and the toes point up. Do another *temps levé* while bringing both feet into the 6th position, then stomp on right leg.	Open arms *à la seconde,* palms open and up.
	Do one *pirouette en dedans* to the right, the left leg lifted to *passé* with a turned-in knee. Finish	Close arms *en avant.*

	pirouette in 6th position.	
38–41	Repeat Step 3 to other side.	
42–49	Repeat Step 2a. This time the boys do the *pas de basques* around the girls, who are now kneeling on the floor.	
50–52	Stand up and move with quick running steps into a wide circle, facing clockwise.	Girls and boys give each other left (right) hand, forearms resting on each other.

Step 4.

53–68	Repeat Step 1, moving in a large circle to the right. After completion of circle, couples form lines on both sides of the stage and turn upstage to welcome the Burgomaster.	Boys hold girls' forearms. Bring outside arm *en avant*, *à la seconde*, and *en haut*. During the *pas de basques*, wave the outside arm back and forth over the head twice.

Step 5.

69–76	The Burgomaster enters from location 3, greeting dancers to left and right.	
77–80	Steps to a girl on the right side and kisses her.	
81–84	Walks over to a girl on the other side and repeats. Invites girls to dance with him.	
85–88	Stomp into 4th position *effacé devant* with right foot, then step with left foot to the right and do a *ballonné* to *effacé devant* while doing a small *temps levé* on left leg. Bring the right foot back to *sur le cou-de-pied devant*. Repeat twice in same direction. Spring into 2nd position, toes and knees turned in, 1/2 toe; click heels together and pause.	Arms hooked at elbow.

Step 5a. (repeat of music)

73–76   All step on left leg into *demi-plié* and brush the right leg *devant*, stretched. Bring right leg next to left into *demi* 1/2 toe, lifting left leg slightly and placing it next to right. Accent is on 1st count, as in a waltz.
Repeat Step 5a three times, moving backward in a line to the right, completing a full circle.

Step 5b.

77–80   Repeat Step 5a with two more girls joining the line.

81–84   Repeat Step 5a to the left, moving backward, counterclockwise.

Step 5c.

85–88   Two girls from the right line bring the "dizzy" Burgomaster to a table to the right in corner 1.

Step 6.

89–92   Girls only, moving sideways in front of boys: Girl's hands in hip position; look at partner.

Step on right full foot, do a *temps levé* on the right, lifting the left leg with knee bent and turned in to *passé*. Bring left leg back to 6th position next to right.
Repeat twice.
Turn abruptly to the left and face the boy, who has been walking behind the girl.

| 93–96 | Girl faces boy and places hands on his shoulders. He lifts her and turns her around once. | |
| 97–104 | Repeat Step 6 with the girl moving to the other side of the boy. Execute lift to other side. | Girl's hands in hip position; look at partner |

Step 7.

| 105–108 | Boys alone move from side to side in *failli, glissade, cabriole:* In the *cabriole* the right (left) leg goes to *effacé en l'air,* the other leg is bent at the knee and the toes touch the right (left) leg in *passé* position. | Arms *à la seconde,* then extend right arm in *seconde,* left arm *en haut* (or reverse). |
| 109–112 | Land and bring legs together with a *soutenu en dedans.* Repeat Step 7 to other side. | Arms move *en haut* and back to *à la seconde.* |

Step 8. *(repeat of music)*

	Franz or solo boy alone, moves diagonally from location 1 to 3:	
105–108	Step into *arabesque* with right leg, *chassé* to location 3.	Right arm *en avant* at eye level; left arm slightly behind left shoulder.
	Do a *double saut de basque* with knees tucked under body. Land at stage center facing forward.	Arms *en haut.* Open arms *à la seconde;* then bring them to hip position.
	Chassé en arrière toward location 3 with left leg, then turn to the left to 4th position, left foot in front, right leg *pointe tendue en arrière.* *Coupé* with right leg and:	

109–112	Step into *arabesque* toward location 3 with left leg, *chassé* toward 1, do a *double saut de basque*, then join partner.	Arm movements as before.

Step 9.

113–116	All couples form a large circle in center of stage:	
	Step on right leg *demi-plié*, lift left leg from knee *demi en arrière*, kick left toes behind on floor. Do one *temps levé* on right leg. Repeat 3 times.	Clasp hands at wrist behind body.
117–120	Walk 4 steps to form a circle, boys on inside facing in, girls on outside facing out. Boys go into slight kneebend.	Large arm movement over *en avant*, *en haut*, then opening to *seconde*. Boys clasp each other's wrists.
	Girls, with help of both hands on boys' shoulders, sit on boys' lowered arms.	
121–128	Boys lift girls and walk around in *balancé* (waltz step).	
129–132	Boys stop and walk in opposite direction, still carrying girls.	
	Girls get down and stand briefly in 6th position.	Arms *à la seconde*, palms open.
	Boys stand in 6th position.	Raise arms *en haut*.
133–136	All do a *temps levé* and run to form a half circle around Franz (lead boy) and his partner.	
	Boys do a *soutenu en dedans* and go down onto left knee.	Arms *en haut*, then into waist position.
	Girls do a *soutenu en dedans* and face boy (toward location 2) in 6th position.	

MAZURKA—STEP 9

Step 10.

137–152	Girls step sideways to right and close left to right foot, stomping strongly 5 times. Boys clap hands twice. Girls stomp 5 times. Boys clap once. Girls stomp twice. Boys clap once. Repeat Step 10 twice.	Hands in hip position. Look at boys, flirting.
153–154	Offer each other hands to get up. Turn around with tiny steps on 1/2 toe, facing each other.	One arm on partner's waist, other stretched *en haut*.
155–158	All couples run back to corner 3 and form two lines, as at the beginning of the Mazurka, but facing corner 1, toward the Burgomaster.	Arms over *en haut* to hip position.

Step 11.

159-166	Take three Mazurka steps toward location 1, starting with right leg.	Outside arm gradually goes to *en haut*, other arm rests on partner's arm.
	Do a *coupé* and a *pas de basque* who lifted knees in a 1/2 turn so that partners face each other.	Arms over *en haut* to hip.
	Step with right (left) leg *croisé devant* and do a *cabriole* with stretched legs toward location 3. Repeat step and *cabriole*.	Arms cross *en avant* when legs do, open to *seconde* and cross again when legs do, then open to *seconde*, palms up.
	Do two *cabrioles*, with no step between, toward 1 (sideways), *sauté* into 2nd position with 1/2 turn to face 1.	Wrists bent, palms down; bend head slightly forward.
	Click heels in 1/2 toe position.	Lift head and turn palms up.

170

| 167–174 | Repeat Step 11, starting with left leg. | |

Step 12.

175–176	Make a 1/2 turn to the left, stepping onto left leg in *demi-plié*, right leg extended *en arrière*, heels up, toes touching the floor.	Hands in hip position.
	Sauté, turn body to the right to the open leg (now in *effacé devant*), right toes pointing up, right heel touching the floor.	Open arms *à la seconde*, palms up.
	Shift full weight onto right leg, placing the foot on full sole, *demi-plié*, extending the left leg *en arrière*, toes only touching the floor. Bring left shoulder toward right side, *sauté*, and turn body towards left leg in *effacé devant*, toes up, heel only on floor.	Hands in hip position. Open arms to *à la seconde*, palms open.
177–178	*Sauté* into 6th position and do one *pirouette en dedans*, with turned-in knee.	Arms *en avant*.

Step 13.

| 179–182 | Boys go into a *grand plié* on right leg, opening left leg *à la seconde* on the floor. Stand up and take 3 small running steps.

Repeat, completing one full turn. | Girls support the boys' kneebend by placing their forearms under those of the boys. Boys hold partners' hip with right arm. |

Step 14.

| 183–186 | Repeat Step 12 with 2 *pirouettes*. | |

Step 15.

	187–190		Repeat Step 13.

Step 16.

	191	*1*	All couples *relevé* onto 1/2 toe briefly.	Arms *en haut.*

Step 17.

		2	Boys go onto left knee in *effacé devant*, girls step toward boys.	Left arm *en haut*, right arm *à la seconde*, palms open.

Step 18.

	192		Girls place left leg on boys' right knee.	Left arm *à la seconde*, right arm *en haut.*

THE MAZURKA

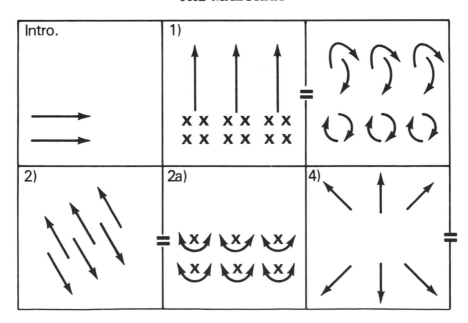

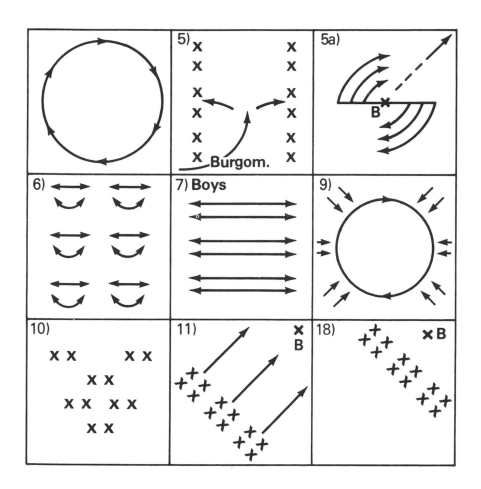

MAZURKA FROM *COPPÉLIA*

LÉO DELIBES

175

CHARACTER DANCE

10. A Betrothal Dance

The Betrothal Dance is a wedding dance for one couple. The one described here is from the third act of the ballet *Coppélia*. It takes place before the wedding, and the dancers are coy, happy, and flirtatious, with much pantomime. The Betrothal Dance has various patterns and is an eastern European custom, but the dance does not show any particular national character.

BETROTHAL DANCE

From *Coppélia*, Act III   Choreography by J. Pagels
Music by L. Delibes   For one couple

2/4

Girl starts from location 8, facing 6, Boy starts from location 6, facing 8. Both have hands in hip position and lean forward.

Step 1

Bars	1–8	Take 20 running steps to reach center stage and run around each other. Kick heels high.	Boy offers his arm; girl puts her arm through his.

Step 2.

	*and**	Step on right leg into *demi-plié* and bring left leg to *croisé devant* of right with small *temps levé*.	Outside arm in hip position; look at each other.

*All steps in the Betrothal Dance start on the third eighth note of the bar.

9–12	*Temps levé* and brush left leg to *effacé* back.	
	Do a *pas de bourrée* with left leg, behind, side, front.	Look left and then right.
	Swing right leg in *demi-rond de jambe en dedans* over left leg with a *temps levé*. Finish with right in front of left.	Look over right shoulder.
	Pas de bourrée with back toward location 4: Place right leg in front of left, opening left *croisé* back; close right to left.	
	Swing left leg in *demi-rond de jambe en dedans* over right with a *temps levé*.	Look over left shoulder.
	Pas de bourrée with back toward location 3: Close left leg to right, opening right to *croisé en arrière;* close left to right.	
12–16	Repeat Step 2 to other side.	

Step 3.

		Girl moves to the right, facing 6; boy to the left, facing 8:	Bend body well forward.
	and	Do a *temps levé* on the left leg, lifting right knee high.	Left arm in front of forehead, slightly covering eyes; right arm *seconde*.
16–24		Do a *temps levé* on the right leg, lifting left knee high (Photo 114).	
		Repeat right and left.	
		Repeat same steps facing forward but moving backward.	Reverse arms.
		Repeat same steps moving backward toward each other; boy facing location 6, girl facing 8.	Reverse arms.
		Do two *temps levé* as before, turn	Open arms as though

114

to face each other, and stamp 3 times.

hugging; place hands on partner's shoulders.

Step 4.

24-26 — Turn so that boy faces location 1; girl faces 3:
Do a *temps levé* on the left leg, bringing right leg in *frappé* toward location 1 and back to the calf.
Place right leg in 6th position to the left.
Repeat with left leg.

Step 4a.

26–28 — Turn body on the diagonal and *echappé* to 4th position *croisé* without turning the feet out; close.
Echappé to other corner; close.
Repeat Step 4a both sides.

Shoulders move opposite to the working leg.

28–30 — Repeat Step 4.

30–32 — Repeat Step 4a, doing the *échappés* in a circular movement. Finish standing next to each other.

Step 5.

32–36	Boy and girl immediately do a *failli, glissade, demi assemblé* to 3rd position toward location 1. Girl jumps up, supported by boy, who lifts her straight up while she does one *tour en l'air*.	Arms *à la seconde*. Girl's arm *en haut*.
	Boy places girl on floor and they walk in a circle around each other, with accent on the first step: right leg *demi-plié*, left leg closing behind right, etc. (Photo 115).	Outside hands at the neck, inside arms stretched out to partner. Boy and girl look at each other.

115

Step 5a.

36–40	Repeat Step 5 to the other side, toward location 2. After placing girl on the floor, boy starts as before and girl runs away toward location 8.

Step 6.

and	Boy and girl face each other: Boy makes a reverence: Do a *demi-plié en arrière* with left leg, heel only on the floor.	Arms open *à la seconde*.

116

41–48   Rise, stand in 6th position, and indicate love for girl.

Boy's right hand to his heart, head inclined and looking at girl. Beckon to girl with right index finger; left hand in hip position.

Girl stands half turned away from boy, shoulders lifted shyly (Photo 116).

Boy nods his head at girl. Girl's hands clasped in front.
Girl looks over shoulder at boy.
Girl looks away, gesturing to audience with hands, "He means me."
Girl looks back at boy.

Girl runs to boy at center stage, at first hesitatingly, then fast.

Boy and girl embrace, bending upper body forward, and kiss.

Step 7.

Boy stands with left leg *allongé en arrière*, right leg in *demi-plié*. Girl sits on his right knee with her legs and knees together and they hug each other. Boy lifts girl at the waist and transfers her to his left knee; then they hug each other again.
Boy lifts girl and places her on floor, next to him, facing location 5.

Step 8.

56–60	Step on left leg, *effacé* toward location 2, and do a *temps levé*.	Left arm in hip position, right arm *ev avant* toward 2.
	Swing right leg in *demi rond de jambe dedans* over left leg. Do a *pas de bourrée:* Place right leg in front of left, open left back, and close right to left, still facing 2. *Cabriole croisé en arrière* with left leg brushing out, right beating. Land on right leg in *demi-plié*, left leg *demi en l'air*.	
	With accent on first step, boy and girl each walk in a small circle.	Outside hand at the neck, inside on hip.
60–64	Repeat Step 8 to other side.	

Step 9.

| 64–70 | Face each other on the diagonal at stage center, boy with back to audience. Do an *arabesque demi-plié*, outside leg lifted.
Hop around in a circle 3 times. Disengage on 14th hop, and change position to opposite direction.
Repeat, hopping 5 times in a circle, then disengage. Stand next to each other facing location 5. | Hold each other at the waist with arm around partner's back. |

Step 9a.

| 70–74 | Stand in 6th position, lift onto 1/2 toe, then lift right knee and turn body slightly toward location 2. Place right toes back on floor next to left. | Head down to toes. Arms open left and right to *seconde*. |

117

	Turn body toward location 1 (Photo 117). Lift knee so that foot comes off the floor, and do a *demi-plié* with right leg.	Both arms go to other side.

Repeat, stepping back on left foot in 1/2 toe and lifting right leg as in a turned-in *sur le cou-de-pied*, etc. (The knees must remain tightly together.)
Repeat Step 9a three times.

Step 10.

74–78	Face each other, and moving in a circle over locations 1, 8, 4, etc., do 5 Waltz steps turning each other, lifting the knees, and hopping slightly. Boy lifts girl high over his head, turns once, and places her back on floor facing 5.	Hold partner's waist.

Step 11.

78–80	Stand next to each other, girl on right side: In 6th position, do a *demi-plié* on the left leg while right leg is	Arms *à la seconde.* Move both arms to the right over *en bas*.

188

brushed out to *à la seconde en l'air*.

Bring right leg back to 6th position, lifting left leg in 1/2 toe.

Both arms *en bas*.

Repeat left, right, and left.

Arms move to left, right, and left.

Step 12. Finale

80–82

Girl does a *chaîné* toward location 1.

Boy holds her left arm and pulls her to him. He lifts her and sets her on his right knee. His left leg is stretched back. They hug and kiss.

Open arms.

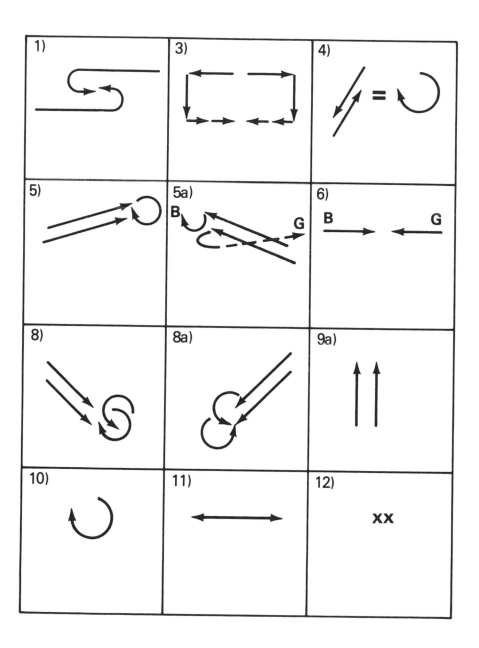

L'HYMEN FROM *COPPÉLIA*

LÉO DELIBES

GLOSSARY

This glossary is not intended to give a full description of the steps and their variations but merely to help those readers who are not familiar with French ballet terms.

For further information see Gail Grant, *Technical Manual and Dictionary of Classical Ballet* (New York: Dover Publications, Inc., 1967).

en l'air	In the air. A movement in the air, such as a jump, or a movement in the air of the working leg while standing on the supporting leg.
allongé	Outstretched, as in extended *arabesque*.
arabesque	With the weight on one leg (in *demi-plié* or straight leg), the other leg is extended and stretched out behind the body at a given angle.
en arrière	Backward; a step or movement to the rear.
attitude	With the weight on one leg (in *demi-plié* or straight leg), the other is lifted behind the body with the knee bent. Preferably, the knee should be in line with the corresponding shoulder, and the foot should not be higher than the knee. *Attitude en avant:* forward attitude.
en avant	Forward; indicates a step or movement that goes forward; in front of the body (opposite the chest).
ballonné	Ball-like. Stand in 5th position, right foot back and *demi-plié:* Jump into the air, brushing the right leg out into a *grand* or *petit battement* in any given direction and bring the right leg into a *sur le cou-de-pied* position in front or behind the left leg. The left leg is stretched during the jump.
en bas	Low, indicating a low position, usually of the arms.
battement, grand or *petit*	Literally "beating," a large or small beat. The working leg is lifted into the air at a given angle and direction with the knee straight.
cabriole	From the Italian "capriola"; a goatlike step. There are many forms of the cabrioles. Generally it involves a jump during which the legs beat against each other in the air. Stand in 5th position, right leg in front. Brush the right leg to *effacé devant*, while jumping off the floor from the left leg. The right leg executes a *battement* and is beaten by the left leg from behind. After the *battement* the left leg descends to the floor, and the right leg is held open or closed in. In some character dances, cabrioles are executed with the heels or with the toes.
cambré	Literally "arched." The body is bent from the waist to the side or front.
chaîné	Chain (or links of a chain). A series of turns, usually *en diagonale*. Step from one foot onto the other, each time doing half a turn.
chassé	Literally "chased"; a hunting step. (Actually one leg chases the other.) The step can be done in many directions: for instance, stand in 5th position, right foot in

195

front, *demi-plié*, and slide the right foot to 4th position *en avant*. The weight of the body is now shifted to the foot in front, which sinks into *demi-plié*. Now spring off the right foot into the air while bringing the left leg to the right leg, which immediately goes into a *sur le cou-de-pied* position in front of the left leg to start the next *chassé*.

en cloche	Like a bell. Refers to a *grand* or *petit battement*, where the working leg passes through the first position front and back.
contretemps	Counter beating. Stand in 4th position, right foot *croisé devant* and *pointe tendue*. Step onto right foot in *demi-plié*, swing the left leg in *demi rond de jambe* across the right leg, do a slight beat as the legs pass each other (optional), bring the left leg into a *demi-plié*, and open the right leg in *effacé devant*.
sur le cou-de-pied	Literally "on the neck of the foot," meaning the ankle, sometimes referred to as the instep. One foot is placed on the ankle of the other, the heel forward, the instep arched over the ankle of the supporting leg and the toes pointing down and to the back, actually wrapping the foot around the other ankle.
coupé	Literally "cut"; the cutting in or out of or between steps; an interrupting movement that often starts from *sur le cou-de-pied*.
croisé	Crossed. A direction of the feet, legs, body, or arms. For instance, the right leg may cross the center line of the body front or back, or may cross over or behind the supporting left leg.
en croix	In the shape of a cross. For instance, a *battement* to the front, side, back, and side again, all with the same working leg.
en dedans	Inward, indicating the direction of a movement, turn, etc. In a *pirouette*, for instance, turn on the left leg to the left side, or on the right leg to the right side.
en dehors	Outward; the opposite of *dedans*.
demi	Literally "half"; as in *demi-plié*, a half bend.
derrière	Behind, back; usually referring to the placement of arms or legs, or a movement to the rear.
devant	In front; the opposite of *derrière*.
développé	Developed, to unfold. An unfolding movement of arm and leg, usually in slow motion (but not necessarily).
écarté	Separated, thrown wide apart. A movement in which the shoulders, legs, and arms are *en diagonale* and open, and the head is turned to one of the corners.
échappé	Escaping or slipping movement. For instance, stand in 5th position *demi-plié*, right leg in front; slide both legs at the same time to 2nd position into half-toe and then slide both legs back into 5th position, right leg now behind left and *demi-plié*. The *échappé* can be done in many directions and positions, as well as with a jump.
éffacé	Shaded. A body placement in which the dancer stands at an oblique angle to the audience, the body in an *épaulement* that is open to the audience between the front and side directions (or back and side directions).
emboîté	Literally "fitted together"; interwoven. Steps or foot movements fitted together. For instance, stand in 5th position *demi-plié*, right foot in front. Jump off the floor and bring the left foot forward, bent at the knee in a *sur le cou-de-pied* position. From this position jump lightly off the floor and bring the other leg forward into the same position. The step travels toward a given direction and is at times *en tournant;* with a half turn of the body for each change of leg.

épaulement	Shouldering. The placement of the shoulders in relation to the body, generally corresponding to the position of the legs. For instance, with the right leg in front, the right shoulder will be brought forward and the heal will be turned toward the right shoulder. (There are few exceptions.)
en face	Full face, opposite. A movement or position facing the audience.
failli	Giving way. For instance, stand in 5th position with the right foot in front, *épaulement, demi-plié*. Jump into the air, turning the body to *effacé* and holding both legs together for a moment. Then open the back (left) leg, as in a *grant jeté* or *sissonne*. As the right leg lands in *demi-plié*, slide the left through 1st position to 5th and to 4th position *en avant*, into a *demi-plié*.
flic-flac, or *flic*	A "flicking" movement, similar to a *frappé*, with the working leg moving toward the supporting leg; or a movement like a *petit fouetté*. Stand in 5th position, right leg in front. Open the left leg to a *demi à la seconde* position, "flic" it, as in a *frappé*, inward and across the lower right leg (sometimes with a half turn). The toes brush the floor briefly in the "flic" movement, the knee of supporting leg is stiff and the heel is lifted only a quarter of the way off the floor. The "flac" is the continuation of the movement to the right. The left leg, with bent knee, crosses behind the right leg, brushing the floor briefly and completing the turn.
fouetté	Literally "whipped"; the whipping of a leg around the body, or the whipping movement of the body itself. There are two important *fouettés*—one is a jump in a variety of directions; the other is a turn. For instance, to execute a *grand fouetté en tournant* jump into the air from an *effacé* position, brushing the right leg out in a *grand battement*. Change the body direction in the air suddenly with a half turn and land in an *arabesque* on the left leg. A *fouetté (pirouette)* is usually done in a series of turns, whipping the working leg to *à la seconde* while stretching the supporting leg from *demi-plié* to *relevé*. The working leg does a *rond de jambe* while the body completes the turn, finishing on the supporting leg in *demi-plié* and opening the working leg to *croisé devant, en avant*, or *à la seconde*.
frappé	Literally "struck," beating. Starting from *à la seconde pointe tendue*, the right leg beats the left in *sur le cou-de-pied devant* and opens again to *à la seconde* with a sharp thrust, brushing the toes over the floor (this varies with different ballet methods) and then extending the foot fully to *seconde*. May be done in any given direction or *en tournant*, with *relevé*, etc.
glissade	Gliding. Stand in 5th position, *demi-plié*, right foot in front. Brush the left leg over the floor to *à la seconde*, and lift the leg slightly off the floor. With a small *sauté* (optional) shift the weight of the body onto the left leg, which is placed into *demi-plié*; maintain the original position with the right leg. Now close the right leg in 5th position in front of (or behind) the left. There are several different *glissades* in many directions.
grand	Large, big, deep; as in *grand pliés*.
en haut	High, indicating an arm position slightly in front of the head and above.
la jambe	The leg.
jeté	Thrown step. Stand in 5 position, *demi-plié*, with the right leg behind. Brush the right leg over the floor *à la seconde* and jump off the floor from the left leg. The extended right leg lands in *demi-plié*; the left leg finishes in *sur le cou-de-pied* behind (or in front). *Grand jeté* is a large jump from one leg onto the other, forming an *arabesque* in the air.

Grand jeté en tournant: Do a *grand battement en avant* with the right leg, jumping off the floor from the left. Make a half (or full) turn in the air with the legs passing each other, and land on the right leg in *demi-plié*, facing the direction from which you started, the left leg extended behind in an *arabesque.*

pas Step.

pas de basque Basque step. It has many variations, jumped or gliding, with legs and knees turned out or in. For instance, stand in 5th position, *demi-plié*, with the right leg in front. Bring the right leg in a semicircle from the front to the side while jumping lightly off the left leg. Transfer the body weight to the right leg and bring the left leg to 5th position and then to 4th position, or through *sur le cou-de-pied* or *passé* to the front and 4th position. Transfer the weight to the front leg and close the back leg into 5th position behind.
This step can be executed sideways, forward, backward, in a circle, or *en tournant* and is at home in most European and Eastern folk dances.

pas de bourrée Literally "stuffed." Stand in 4th position, right foot in front, left foot *pointe tendue* behind. Bring the left foot in *relevé* to 5th position behind the right, open the right leg to 2nd position in 1/2 toe and close the left leg in front of the right into 5th position *demi-plié.*
There are many *pas de bourrées*, such as *en tournant*, *changé*, *en avant*, and *en arrière*, usually starting with a 5th position, then a 2nd, and then a 5th again, or with a 4th position in between.

pas de chat A cat step, catlike. Stand in 5th position, right leg behind, *demi-plié*. Jump off the floor bringing the right leg to *passé* and immediately lifting the left foot to the right knee, while still in the air. Descend, landing on the right leg, then close the left leg in front in 5th position.

pas de ciseaux Scissor step; the legs execute a scissor movement while in the air. For instance, do a *cabriole effacé devant*, but instead of beating the legs together, pass them quickly front and back, before landing on the floor on one leg. The same step can be done in character dance by jumping off the ground, bending with legs at the knee but keeping the knees tightly together, and opening the lower legs front and back.

pas marché Marching step, actually three steps, in which the accent is on the first step, the downbeat, or on the *développé* (the stretched, sliding out of the forward, moving leg): Step forward on the left leg, hitting the floor strongly. Almost simultaneously, stretch the right leg in a *développé devant* and take a normal walking step. Follow with a walking step with the left leg. Repeat, starting with a strong forward step (stomp) with the right leg.

passé Literally "passed"; usually the passing of a leg from one position to another, such as the foot of the working leg passing the knee of the supporting leg. Or, the position in which the foot of the working leg is held at the knee of the supporting leg.

pas tombé Falling, indicating a fall of the body, forward or in any other direction, usually from one leg onto the other.

petit Small, little.

pirouette Spin, whirl, a turn on the floor with the supporting leg in *relevé*, the working leg in a *passé* or some other position.

pivot A point; to turn, a pointing movement, to point, to step on.

plié, demi or *grand* Bent, a kneebend with the knees turned out (turned in, in character dances).

pointe tendue	Pointed or stretched, as in a *battement pointe tendue*, in which the working leg is stretched and the toes pointed (at the floor).
port de bras	Carriage of the arms. The movement of the arms or exercises of the arms to any given position and direction.
relevé	Raised, raising the body onto half toe or full point.
retiré	Literally "withdrawn"; the leg is raised so that the toes touch the side of the knee of the supporting leg.
rond de jambe, à terre or *en l'air*	Literally "rounding the leg"; a circular movement of the leg on the floor or in the air.
sauté	Jumped, jumping. A jump.
à la seconde	To second position. A movement of the leg or arm to the side of the body.
soutenu	Sustained, a sustained movement. *Soutenu en tournant* (sustained movement with a turn, inward or outward): Stand in 5th position, left leg in front, *demi-plié*. Open the right leg to *à la seconde*, bring the right leg in *rond de jambe à terre* to *croisé devant* over the left leg rising onto half toe at the same time. Continue turning the body over the left shoulder *(en dedans)* on both legs for one full turn. Finish in 5th position, left leg in front, *demi-plié*.
temps	Time, step, movement.
temps levé	Literally "time related"; a raised movement, a small jump, a hop. An upward spring off one foot (or both), while the other foot is placed in an extended *arabesque, attitude,* or *sur le cou-de-pied* position.
à terre, or *par terre*	On the ground.

BIBLIOGRAPHY

Beaumont, Cyril W. *A French-English Dictionary of Technical Terms Used in Classical Ballet*. London: C. W. Beaumont, 1966.

Buday, György. *Dances of Hungary*. London: Parrish, 1950.

Galanti, Bianca. *Dances of Italy*. London: Parrish, 1950.

Grant, Gail. *Technical Manual and Dictionary of Classical Ballet*. New York: Dover, 1967.

Jankovic, Lyubica, and Jankovic, Danica. *Dances of Yugoslavia*. New York: Crown Publishers, 1952.

Lubinova, Mila. *Dances of Czechoslovakia*. London: Parrish, 1949.

Sorell, Walter. *The Dance through the Ages*. New York: Grosset & Dunlap, 1967.

Sparger, Celia. *Anatomy and Ballet: A Handbook for Teachers of Ballet*, 5th ed. New York: Theatre Arts Books, 1970.

Tkachenko, Tamara. *Soviet Dances*. Selected and translated by Joan Lawson from *Folk Dances of the U.S.S.R.* (Moscow, 1954). London: Imperial Society of Teachers of Dancing, 1964.

Wolska, Helen. *Dances of Poland*. New York: Crown Publishers, 1952.